FAMII WALKS

CHILTERNS - SOUTH

Nick Moon

This book is one of a series of two which provide a comprehensive coverage of walks throughout the whole of the Chiltern area. The walks included vary in length from 1.7 to 5.5 miles, but are mainly in the 3- to 5-mile range which is ideal for families with children, less experienced walkers or short winter afternoons.

Each walk text gives details of nearby places of interest and is accompanied by a specially drawn map of the route which also indicates local pubs and a skeleton road network.

The author, Nick Moon, has lived in or regularly visited the Chilterns all his life and has, for 25 years, been an active member of the Chiltern Society's Rights of Way Group, which seeks to protect and improve the area's footpath and bridleway network. Thanks to the help and encouragement of the late Don Gresswell MBE, he was introduced to the writing of books of walks and has since written or contributed to a number of publications in this field.

OTHER PUBLICATIONS BY NICK MOON

Family Walks
Family Walks 1 : Chilterns - South : Book Castle 1997
Family Walks 2 : Chilterns - North : due 1998

Chiltern Walks Trilogy
Chiltern Walks 1: Hertfordshire, Bedfordshire and
                   North Buckinghamshire:
                   Book Castle (new edition) 1996
Chiltern Walks 2 : Buckinghamshire:
                   Book Castle (new edition) 1997
Chiltern Walks 3 : Oxfordshire and West Buckinghamshire:
                   Book Castle (new edition) 1996

Oxfordshire Walks
Oxfordshire Walks 1: Oxford, The Cotswolds and The Cherwell
                     Valley: Book Castle 1994
Oxfordshire Walks 2: Oxford, The Downs and The Thames Valley:
                     Book Castle 1995

Other Complete Books
Walks for Motorists: Chilterns (Southern Area):
                      Frederick Warne 1979
Walks for Motorists: Chilterns (Northern Area):
                      Frederick Warne 1979
Walks in the Hertfordshire Chilterns: Shire 1986

First published July 1997
by The Book Castle
12 Church Street, Dunstable, Bedfordshire.

Printed in Great Britain by Antony Rowe Ltd., Chippenham, Wilts.

ISBN 1 871199 38 7

Contents

FAMILY WALKS 1 : CHILTERNS - SOUTH
LIST OF WALKS

POSSIBLE LONGER WALKS PRODUCED BY COMBINING WALKS DESCRIBED IN THE BOOK

Walks	Miles	Km
3 + 5	8.8	14.2
10 + 11	10.7	17.2
14 + 15	9.4	15.1

Cover photograph : © Nick Moon. Approaching Hambleden (Walk 24).

Introduction

This book of walks is one of two covering the whole of the Chilterns from the Goring Gap on the River Thames to the Hitchin Gap in North Hertfordshire. The part covered by this volume is that roughly south of a line from Princes Risborough in the west through Amersham to Rickmansworth in the east and so includes the whole of the Oxfordshire Chilterns, a substantial part of the Buckinghamshire Chilterns and the southern tip of the Hertfordshire Chilterns.

To the west, the area is bounded by the high Chiltern escarpment with its fine views, its variety of open downland, woodland and scrub and its pleasant foothills with views towards the ridge; to the south, there is the Thames Valley with its beautiful scenery and picturesque riverside towns, while to the east is the Colne Valley, now a regional park, with the Grand Union Canal with its colourful narrowboats and numerous gravel lakes frequented by a rich assortment of waterfowl.

Within this area there is also a wide variety of landscapes. To the south of the Wallingford - Henley road is the most heavily-wooded part of the Chilterns which, though less hilly than some other areas, offers particularly quiet walks through woods and remote clearings and hamlets. Further to the north and to the west of High Wycombe is the characteristic Chiltern landscape of high ridges and deep, steep-sided, mostly dry bottoms liberally scattered with woodland and brick-and-flint cottages including some of the finest walking areas in the Chilterns such as Bix Bottom and the Wormsley, Turville, Hambleden and Hughenden valleys, while to the north of Beaconsfield there is the quiet and well-wooded but less hilly plateau offering fine rural walks less than 30 miles from Central London. To the south of Beaconsfield is another heavily-wooded area including the nationally renowned Burnham Beeches with their ancient beech trees and the surprisingly unspoilt rural villages of Hedgerley and Fulmer. Finally in the northeast of the area are the Misbourne and Chess valleys where characteristic Chiltern scenery is combined with the special charms of small natural waterways and active measures are underway to enhance the landscape and its recreational value.

The basic walks in this book are in the 3 - 5.5 mile range which is ideal for families, less experienced walkers or short winter afternoons and there are a number of shorter versions given which may be preferable for those with younger children or when time is short. In addition, details of several possible combinations of walks of up to 10.7 miles are provided for those wishing to take a longer walk but those requiring more are advised to try the ´Chiltern Walks` series by the same author which contain basic walks in the 5 - 10 mile range, as well as combination walks of up to 23 miles.

Details of how to reach the starting points by car and where to park are given in the introductory information to each walk and any convenient railway stations are shown on the accompanying plan. As bus services are liable to frequent change, including information in this book might prove more misleading than helpful and so those wishing to reach the walks by bus are advised to obtain up-to-date information from the following sources:-

Buckinghamshire	: Telephone : 0345-382000
Hertfordshire	: Telephone : 0345-244344
Oxfordshire	: Contact : Oxfordshire County Council,
	Public Transport Section,
	Dept. of Planning & Property Services,
	Speedwell House, Speedwell Street,
	Oxford OX1 1SD,
	for a free up-to-date bus map.

All the walks described here follow public rights of way, use recognised permissive paths or cross public open space. As the majority of walks cross land used for economic purposes such as agriculture, forestry or the rearing of game, walkers are urged to follow the Country Code at all times (see page 10). Observing these rules helps prevent financial loss to landowners and damage to the environment, as well as the all-too-frequent and sometimes justified bad feeling towards walkers in the countryside.

While it is hoped that the special maps provided with each walk will assist the user to complete the walks without going astray and skeleton details of the surrounding road network are given to enable walkers to shorten the routes in emergency, it is always advisable to take an Ordnance Survey or Chiltern Society map with you to enable you to shorten or otherwise vary the routes without using roads or get your bearings if you do become seriously lost. Details of the appropriate maps are given in the introductory information of each walk.

As for other equipment, readers are advised that some mud will normally be encountered on most walks particularly in woodland except in the driest weather. However proper walking boots are to be recommended at all times as, even when there are no mud problems, hard ruts or rough surfaces make the protection given by boots to the ankles desirable. In addition, the nature of the countryside makes many Chiltern paths prone to overgrowth, particularly in summer. To avoid resultant discomfort, protective clothing is advisable, especially where specific warnings are given.

In order to assist in coordinating the plans and the texts, all the numbers of path used have been shown on the plans and incorporated into the texts. These numbers, which are also shown on the Chiltern Society's series of footpath maps, consist of the official County Council footpath number with prefix letters used to indicate the parish concerned. It is therefore most helpful to use these when reporting any path problems you may find, together, if possible, with the national grid reference for the precise location of the trouble spot, as, in this way, the problem can be identified on the ground with a minimum of time loss in looking for it. National grid references can, however, only be calculated with the help of Ordnance Survey Landranger, Explorer or Pathfinder maps and an explanation of how this is done can be found in the Key to all Landranger and Explorer maps.

The length of time required for any particular walk depends on a number of factors such as your personal walking speed, the number of hills, stiles, etc. to be negotiated, whether or not you stop to rest, eat or drink, investigate places of interest, for children to play, etc. and the number of impediments such as mud, crops, overgrowth, ploughing, etc. which you encounter, but generally an average speed of between two and two and a half miles per hour (or perhaps one and a half miles per hour with young children) is about right in the Chilterns. It is, however, always advisable to allow extra time if you are limited by the daylight or catching a particular bus or train home in order to avoid your walk developing into a race against the clock.

Should you have problems with any of the paths used on the walks or find that the description given is no longer correct, the author would be most grateful if you could let him have details (c/o The Book Castle), so that attempts can be made to rectify the problem or the text can be corrected at the next reprint. Nevertheless, the author hopes that you will not encounter any serious problems and have pleasure from following the walks.

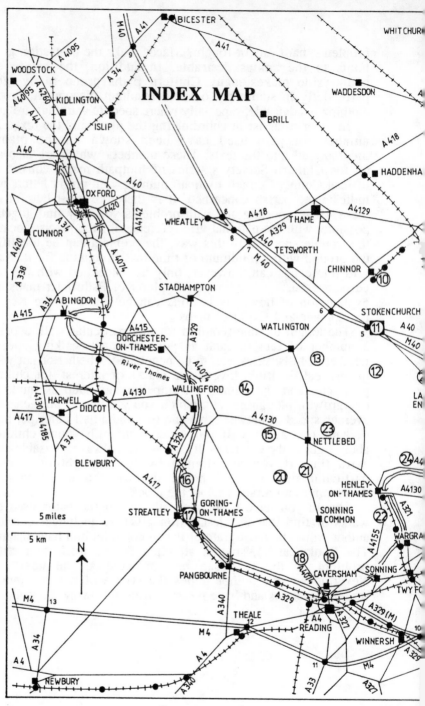

INDEX MAP

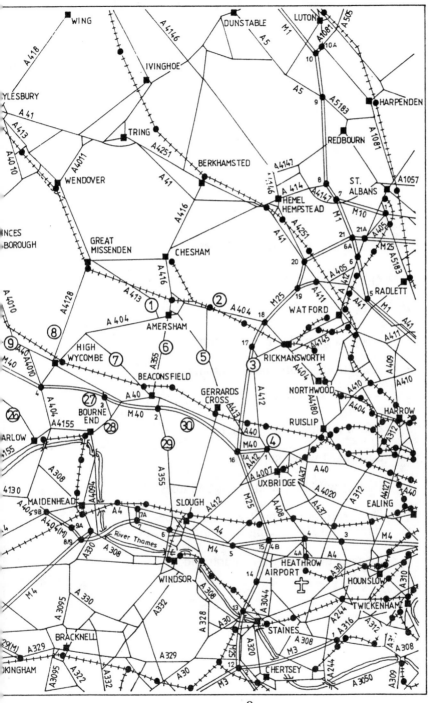

9

Country Code

- Guard against all risk of fire

- Fasten all gates

- Keep dogs under proper control

- Keep to the paths across farmland

- Avoid damaging fences, hedges and walls

- Leave no litter - take it home

- Safeguard water supplies

- Protect wild life, wild plants and trees

- Go carefully on country roads on the right-hand side facing oncoming traffic

- Respect the life of the countryside

WALK 1   Amersham (Shardeloes Park)

Length of Walk: 4.1 miles / 6.6 Km
Starting Point: Shardeloes Park Lodge, west of Amersham.
Grid Ref: SU947978
Maps: OS Landranger Sheet 165
OS Explorer Sheet 3 (or old Pathfinder Sheet 1138 (SU89/99))
Chiltern Society FP Map No.6
How to get there / Parking: Shardeloes Park Lodge, west of Amersham, may be reached from the junction of the A355 and A413 at the foot of Gore Hill on the edge of the town by taking the A413 Amersham Bypass towards Aylesbury. At the second roundabout turn left onto a road signposted to Shardeloes and park in the parking bay on the right near the lodge gates of Shardeloes Park.
Notes: Heavy nettle growth may be encountered in places in the summer months.

Shardeloes, on the crest of a hill above the Misbourne valley to the west of Amersham, was for over 300 years home to the Drake family who played a considerable role in the town's development, building the almshouses in 1657 and the Market Hall, which still dominates the High Street, in 1682 and their importance is reflected by a fine array of family monuments in St. Mary's Church. The old house, where William Tothill (father of thirty-three children) had entertained Elizabeth I, was rebuilt in the Palladian style between 1758 and 1766 for Sir William Drake by Stiff Leadbetter and completed by the later renowned Robert Adam. During landscaping work on its beautiful park excavations to form the lake revealed a Roman villa, thus demonstrating that the site had been inhabited well before Adam de Shardeloes gave his name to the park in the fourteenth century.

The walk first leads you into and through this beautiful park with fine views of the lake and the house with its impressive portico of Corinthian columns. You then continue up the Misbourne valley to the quiet village of Little Missenden where a detour is possible to see one of the oldest churches in the Chilterns. From here you climb through pleasant woodland to

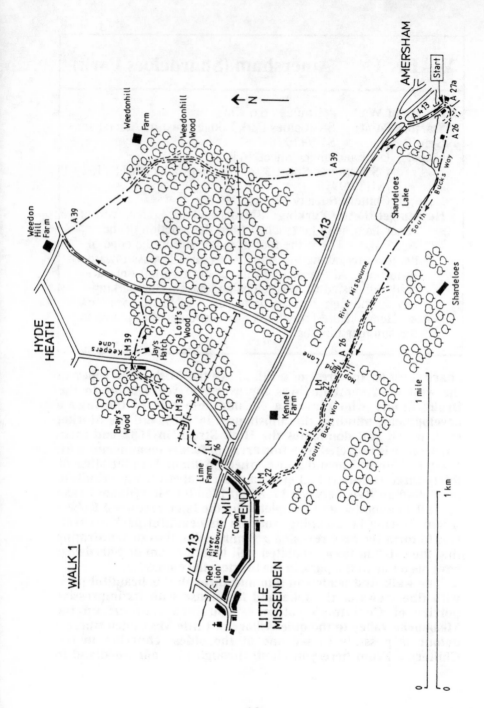

WALK 1

HYDE HEATH

AMERSHAM

Start

LITTLE MISSENDEN

MILL END

'Crown'

'Red Lion'

Lime Farm

Bray's Wood

Keepers Lane

Jay's Hatch

Lott's Wood

Kennel Farm

Weedon Hill Farm

Weedonhill Farm

Weedonhill Wood

Shardeloes Lake

Shardeloes

River Misbourne

South Bucks Way

Mop End Lane

A 413

A 39

A 26

A 27a

LM 39

LM 38

LM 16

LM 22

LM 22

N

0   1 mile

0   1 km

12

the edge of the scattered hilltop village of Hyde Heath before descending through more woodland to reach your starting point.

Starting by the post-box near the lodge gates of Shardeloes Park, take path A27a, part of the South Bucks Way, through the gates. Just past the twin lodges fork right onto path A26 through gates into Amersham Cricket Ground. Where the drive bears right, leave it and go straight on across the cricket field passing left of the pavilion and continuing across a practice field to a gate and kissing-gate. (NB During matches you can avoid the cricket field by following the drive round the back of the pavilion and then bearing half left across the practice field to rejoin the official path at the gate and kissing-gate). Now take a fenced path straight on, soon with Shardeloes Lake visible through the trees to your right, to reach a stile into a parkland field. Here follow a right-hand fence straight on along the shore of the lake soon with a fine view of Shardeloes house on the hillside to your left. At the far end of the field turn left and follow the right-hand fence uphill. After about 50 yards turn right over two stiles and go straight across a parkland field heading for what appears to be the right-hand end of a belt of trees on the next rise, joining a slightly raised track and following it, later with a fence to your left, to reach gates into Mop End Lane. Cross this fenced bridleway and a stile by gates opposite and take path LM22 straight on along a grassy track beside a left-hand hedge. At the far end of the field cross a stile by gates to join a fenced farm road and follow it straight on for a quarter mile to reach a bend in a road at Mill End on the edge of Little Missenden.

Little Missenden, the centre of which is about a third of a mile straight ahead along the road, is particularly notable for having one of the oldest churches in the Chilterns, parts of which date from the tenth century, although like most mediaeval churches it was modified and extended over the centuries with Norman arcades, the fourteenth-century North Chapel and a fifteenth-century tower. Apart from its sheer age, this church is also of interest for its array of mediaeval murals dating from the twelfth to sixteenth centuries. Nearby there is also a Jacobean manor house which was once the home of Dr. Bates, physician to Sir Francis Dashwood and a member of the notorious Hellfire Club who claimed that the stories about the club were ´scandalous and sarcastic fabrications`. That Little Missenden is not only attractive but also a healthy place to live is suggested by the fact that Dr. Bates survived to the age of 98!

If not taking a detour to the village or one of its pubs, leave the South Bucks Way turning right onto the road and follow it crossing the River Misbourne by the seventeenth-century Mill House with its fine wisteria and continuing to the A413. Cross this dual-carriageway carefully and take a service road opposite bearing right. Just past Lime Farm to your left, turn left over a stile onto fenced path LM16. After some 200 yards cross a stile and follow the fenced path bearing right uphill to cross a high footbridge over the railway, once part of the Metropolitan Railway and now part of the Chiltern Line. Having descended the steps on the far side of the railway, turn right over two stiles onto fenced path LM38 leading to a corner of Bray's Wood. Here ignore a stile ahead and bear right through a fence gap into the wood where you bear left and take a waymarked path crossing the wood diagonally, later joining a track which merges from your right and reaching a gate into Keepers Lane.

Cross this road and take path LM39 straight on along the drive to 'Jay's Hatch`, immediately forking left over a stile into a fenced path which soon emerges into a field. Here follow a right-hand hedge straight on to cross a concealed stile into a corner of Lott's Wood. Just inside the wood fork left and follow its inside edge for some 250 yards crossing a stile at one point and later reaching a road. Turn left onto this road and follow it for a third of a mile to a road junction near Hyde Heath.

Here turn right over a stile by gates and take path A39 straight across a field to the near corner of Weedonhill Wood, some 200 yards right of Weedonhill Farm. Cross a stile here to enter the wood then after some 80 yards at a waymarked fork turn right and immediately fork left onto a grassy track down the valley bottom. Follow this track for some 250 yards ignoring a branching track to the left, then at a fork go right onto a track climbing gently along the contours of the hill keeping left at two further forks and eventually reaching a stile leading to a railway level-crossing. Cross the railway carefully then bear half right through line-side scrub to cross a stile into further woodland. In the wood keep left at a fork and take the obvious path downhill to a stile into a field. Here bear right crossing the field diagonally, soon with fine views of Shardeloes on a hillside to your right, to cross a stile in the far corner of the field leading to steps up to a layby on the A413. Cross the dual-carriageway carefully and turn left onto its far verge, soon joining a section of disused road to your right which leads to gates onto the road to Shardeloes. Here turn right for your starting point.

WALK 2   Latimer

Length of Walk: (A) 5.1 miles / 8.2 Km
                         (B) 2.6 miles / 4.1 Km
Starting Point: Parking area in Stony Lane, near Latimer.
Grid Ref: TQ005982
Maps: OS Landranger Sheet 176 or Sheets 165 & 166
         OS Pathfinder Sheet 1139 (TQ09/19) & OS
         Explorer Sheet 3 (or old Pathfinder Sheet 1138
         (SU89/99))
         Chiltern Society FP Map No.5
How to get there / Parking: Stony Lane, Latimer, some
     2.5 miles east of Amersham, may be reached from the
     town by taking the A404 towards Watford ignoring Bell
     Lane, the first turning signposted to Latimer. At the far
     end of Little Chalfont turn left into Stony Lane, sign-
     posted to Latimer and Flaunden, looking out for a large
     unsignposted parking area after 300 yards on your left.
Notes : Heavy nettle growth may be encountered at several
     points on Walk A in the summer months.

Latimer, hidden in the Chess valley a mere half mile from the edge of its suburban neighbour Little Chalfont, remains an idyllic rural backwater with its picturesque cottages ranged around a small triangular green with an old village pump, an obelisk in memory of men killed in the Boer War and a stone memorial to a horse captured by Major General Lord Chesham at the Battle of Boshof in 1900, brought back to England and buried on the green in 1911. On a hilltop above the village is the gaunt-looking Latimer House, seat from 1615 of the Cavendish family (Lords Chesham from 1858). Almost entirely rebuilt in Victorian times, the old house was used in 1647 to imprison Charles I and subsequently hid Charles II before his escape to France. Requisitioned by the Government in 1939 for interrogating prisoners-of-war, Latimer House later became a military staff college until this moved to Greenwich in 1983 and it is now used as a conference centre. Despite the fact that Latimer did not have a church till 1841 and become a separate civil parish till 1898, the village, known till the fourteenth century as Isenhampstead Cheynduit and then as Isenhampstead Latimer, finally losing its

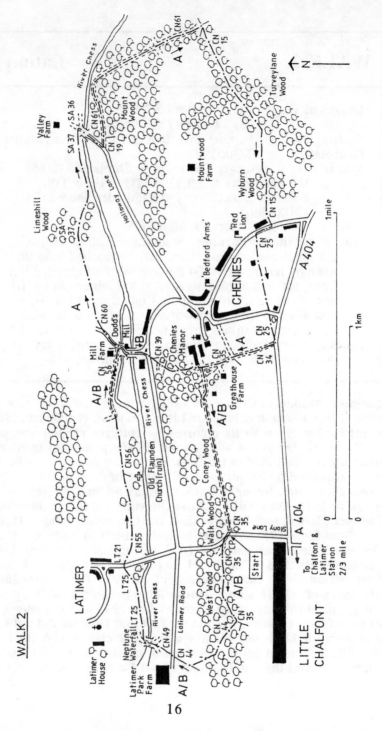

WALK 2

SARRATT

16

first name in the nineteenth century, has been the site of human habitation for some 2000 years as, when Latimer Park Farm was built in the nineteenth century, the site of a substantial Roman villa was discovered dating from about 150 A.D.

Starting from the car park in Stony Lane on a hillside south of the village, both walks lead you through pleasant woodland down into the picturesque Chess valley near Latimer Park Farm, crossing the river below Latimer House near Neptune Waterfall and then proceeding through parkland to the edge of the village before continuing past the site of Flaunden´s old church to Chenies Bottom. From here Walk A continues downstream towards Sarratt and then circles round to skirt the beautiful village of Chenies before rejoining Walk B and continuing with superb views across the Chess valley back to your starting point.

Both walks start from the bottom end of the rough car park in Stony Lane and take this road downhill into Walk Wood. At a right-hand bend leave the road and take bridleway CN35 straight on into West Wood, immediately forking left. Now follow the inside edge of the wood for a quarter mile. Where the bridleway bears left and a stile comes into view ahead, turn right through a fence gap onto path CN44, a sunken way descending through the wood. On nearing its bottom edge, ignore a branching path to your left and bear slightly right leaving the wood by a stile. Now go straight on across a field, with views of Latimer House ahead, passing right of tall chestnut and lime trees to reach the corner of a fence. Here bear half right to reach a kissing-gate in the bottom right-hand corner of the field where you cross Latimer Road, go through a gate opposite and take path CN49 bearing slightly right across a paddock to a gate in the far corner leading to a junction of private roads. Now take path LT25 straight on along a macadam drive over two bridges over the River Chess near Neptune Waterfall with a fine view opening out towards Latimer House on the hilltop ahead.

At the far end of the second bridge turn right over a stile by a gate then go through another gate and follow a right-hand fence along the bank of an attractive artificial lake. On reaching a group of trees, leave the fence and the lake and bear half left across a field to a stile by two road signs on the edge of Latimer village. Cross the road and a stile opposite and take path LT21 beside a left-hand hedge to a stile right of a gate. Now continue across a field passing the corner of a fence then taking worn path CN55 following the contours of the hill and bearing left to join a left-hand fence. At the far end of the field is a copse to your right concealing the ruins of the old church of the Hertfordshire village of Flaunden, a tiny structure built in the shape of a Greek cross in about 1230 and abandoned following its replacement in 1838 by a new church in the hilltop village, over 1 mile away. By a quirk of history, following a recent county boundary change, the old church is now located in Chenies, Bucks! Here take bridleway CN56 straight on crossing a stile by a gate and following a left-hand fence past a pair of oak trees shading the tomb of the Chorleywood brickmaker, William Liberty (1725 - 1777) and his wife Alice. At the far end of the field ignore a footpath and a bridleway to your left, go straight on through a gate and take a track along the bank of an arm of the River Chess to Mill Farm where you bear half left through the farmyard to reach a bend in a road at Chenies Bottom. Here **Walk A** turns left onto the road and omits the next paragraph.

Walk B turns right onto the road crossing two bridges over arms of the Chess and passing Dodd's Mill. Where the road forks, keep right. At a T-junction cross the major road and enter Placehouse Copse, immediately keeping right at a fork and taking path CN39 straight on uphill ignoring a branching track to your right and a crossing path. At a second crossways bear slightly left onto an inconspicuous waymarked path uphill soon leaving the wood by farm buildings on the edge of Chenies. Here take a rough road straight on to a gate then turn right through a second gate onto bridleway CN35 rejoining Walk A. Now read the last paragraph.

At a left-hand bend **Walk A** goes straight on over a stile by a gate onto path CN60 following a right-hand fence along the top of a bank at first, then crossing a field to a stile. Here go straight on to another stile then bear slightly left following a left-hand hedge to a stile at the Hertfordshire boundary into Limeshill Wood. Now take path SA37 straight on through the wood. At the far side of the wood cross a stile and take a fenced path bearing right towards the River Chess. On nearing the riverbank, the path turns left and continues close to the river for nearly a quarter mile to a stile onto a concrete road. Here turn right onto path SA36 crossing a stile by a gate and a footbridge over the Chess beside a ford then take Holloway Lane straight on. At a right-hand bend turn left through a gap by a gate onto path CN19 soon entering Mount Wood. Here cross a stile by a gate and take path CN61 straight on following the contours of the hill through replanted woodland with fine views in places across the Chess valley to your left. After a quarter mile the path bears right and enters mature woodland, through which it continues for more than a third of a mile. Where a field comes into view to your right, ignore a crossing track and keep straight on to a gate and stile into marshland. Here ignore a branching path to your left and continue to a signposted crossways, then turn right over a stile into Turveylane Wood. Ignoring a second stile to your right, take path CN15 straight on up the valley bottom through the wood for over a third of a mile until you eventually bear right and leave the wood through a gap by an old stile. Turn left along the outside edge of the wood to a slight outcrop of woodland then bear half right across a field uphill to a stile near the right-hand corner of Wyburn Wood. Now follow the inside edge of the wood straight on to a stile out of the wood then continue beside a right-hand hedge to a further stile into a fenced path leading to a road at Chenies.

Chenies, which belonged to the Earls and Dukes of Bedford and their predecessors by marriage, the Cheyne family, from the thirteenth century till 1954, is today a picturesque model village largely rebuilt by the Estate in the nineteenth century. Its fine Manor, once known as Chenies Palace, is in part fifteenth-century but mainly dates from 1530 when it was extended by the 1st Earl of Bedford while the fifteenth-century church is noted for the Bedford Chapel dating from 1556 with its superb monuments.

Cross this road and turn right onto its footway. After 120 yards turn left through a kissing-gate onto path CN25 following a right-hand hedge across a recreation ground to a further kissing-gate. Now keep straight on across the next field, gradually diverging from the right-hand hedge to cross a stile in the far hedge then continue along a fenced path past horse paddocks to a stile onto a road. Cross this road and take path CN25 straight on through a copse beside a right-hand hedge to the A404 opposite an ancient painted iron milepost on the old Reading-Hatfield turnpike road. Almost immediately turn right through gates onto path CN34, the drive to Greathouse Farm and follow it with views of Chenies Manor and Church to your right to a junction of drives. Here take bridleway CN35 straight on ignoring a branching path to your left then by farm buildings turn left through a gate rejoining Walk B.

Walks A and B now take fenced bridleway CN35 straight on through a wood ignoring a crossing path. On leaving the wood, go through a gate and wiggle to your right with a fine view towards Latimer opening out ahead. Here ignoring stiles to your right, take the fenced bridleway straight on, passing a seat in memory of Stella Sturch from which you can admire the view. Having passed Coney Wood to your right, Latimer House comes into view later with the village reemerging from behind the wood. On entering Walk Wood, take a track straight on to reach Stony Lane opposite the car park.

19

WALK 3   Maple Cross

Length of Walk: 4.1 miles / 6.6 Km
Starting Point: ´Cross Inn`, Maple Cross.
Grid Ref: TQ033928
Maps: OS Landranger Sheet 176
        OS Pathfinder Sheet 1139 (TQ09/19)
How to get there / Parking: Maple Cross, 2 miles southwest
of Rickmansworth, may be reached from the town or
Junction 17 of the M25 by taking the A412 towards
Uxbridge to Maple Cross. Here, at the traffic lights, turn
right onto a road signposted to The Chalfonts, then
immediately left into a service road where you can park.
Notes: The walked route of path RK11 is currently off-line
in Bottom Wood. Should the correct line be cleared and
waymarked, it will be necessary to go straight on at the
´T-junction` referred to in the text. Heavy nettle growth
may be encountered in places on paths CP7 and RK9 in
the summer months.

Maple Cross, straddling the A412 North Orbital Road in the
Colne valley at the southwestern tip of Hertfordshire, today has a
suburban appearance with its pre-war ribbon development, its
modern housing estates and its industrial estate radiating from a
crossroads by the seventeenth-century ´Cross Inn `. Indeed, a
study of old maps reveals that up to the First World War the
village, whose name is thought to be a corruption of ´Maypole
Cross `, consisted merely of the inn, several farms and a few
cottages. Despite the lack of old buildings, however, Maple Cross
nevertheless has something of architectural interest as the British
headquarters of Nissan on the edge of the village are housed in
some distinctive modern buildings which combine the functional
character of modern western offices with a pagoda-style roof
reminiscent of old Japan.

Despite the inauspicious nature of your starting point, the walk
soon leads you across the M25 into surprisingly quiet open hill
country with fine views, passing through Bottom Wood to enter
Buckinghamshire at Newland Park, where you can take a detour
to visit the Chiltern Open Air Museum. Your return route then
takes you by way of the boundary hamlet of Horn Hill before

dropping with fine views across the Colne valley to reach Maple Cross.

Starting from the road junction near the 'Cross Inn ', take the footway of the A412 northwards. Where the service road ends and the Nissan buildings begin to your right, turn left onto bridleway RK10, the drive to Woodoaks, going through a gate and following a macadam drive. Just past a pair of semi-detached houses leave the drive and bear slightly right across a field to a gate and bridlegate left of a green barn at Woodoaks Farm. Here go straight on between the barns joining a concrete road. Just before a black weatherboarded barn with a tiled roof, turn left onto bridleway RK62, a stony track passing between farm buildings. Now bear half right and follow a left-hand fence and sporadic hedge uphill, entering a hedged lane leading into Ladywalk Wood. Just inside the wood fork right onto a track along the spine of the wood. After about 400 yards, on reaching a bend in a macadam farm road, turn left onto it, rejoining bridleway RK10 and crossing a bridge over the M25.

Now turn right then immediately left over a stile onto path RK11 following a right-hand hedge with fine views to your left across the hills. Where the hedge bears right, leave it and go straight on across the field to cross a stile into Bottom Wood some 100 yards beyond its near corner. Take an obvious path straight on through the wood to a T-junction of paths. Here the de facto line of the path turns right (see **Notes**) and follows a worn path along the valley bottom. By the corner of a field to your right, ignore a branching path to your right. About 50 yards further on at a fork, go left uphill to the top edge of the wood where you bear left along the inside edge of the wood, soon wiggling to your right. By the corner of a field to your right, go right at a fork, still following the inside edge of the wood at first, then bearing left through the wood to reach a stile into a field where there are fine views to your left across the Colne valley towards Harefield and you rejoin the official route of path RK11. Here bear right and follow a right-hand hedge through two fields to a stile into Shire Lane, a bridleway marking the Bucks boundary.

Cross this lane and a stile opposite onto path CP7 entering Newland Park, where the late eighteenth-century mansion and surrounding buildings to the right of the path now serve as a college, following a left-hand fence to cross a macadam drive. Now follow the edge of a fenced sports pitch straight on, then bear slightly right across the playing field to cross a stile left of a wooden electricity pole into a parkland field. Here, if wishing to visit the Chiltern Open Air Museum with its growing collection of architecturally interesting rescued buildings, take a branch of path CP7 straight on along the edge of the field, soon bearing right. Otherwise take the main route of path CP7 bearing half left across the park, passing between the left-hand pair of a line of three oak-trees and left of a pair of conifers to reach a stile into Gorelands Lane.

Cross this road and a stile opposite and take fenced path CP7 past greenhouses to a stile at a path junction. Having crossed this stile, turn left over two more stiles onto path CP9 following a left-hand hedge uphill. At the top of the rise ignore a gate to your left, then leave the hedge and go straight on across the field to cross a stile in a field corner. Now follow a right-hand hedge to a stile into Brallings Lane opposite a cottage. Bear slightly right across this road to cross a rail-stile, then (still on path CP9) bear half right crossing a large field diagonally, soon heading for a pair of cottages at Horn Hill.

At the beginning of the twentieth century Henry Harben, who bought Newland Park together with much of this scattered hamlet in 1903, not only extended his own house but also made plans to transform Horn Hill into a model village and indeed built a fine village hall and twelve new estate cottages. Following his death in 1910 and the outbreak of the First World War, however, his son was forced to abandon the scheme before its completion.

Cross a stile opposite the left-hand cottage and bear slightly left across Shire Lane onto fenced path RK9, left of the entrance to Cross Keys Farm. Follow this path, bearing left then right by the farm, to reach a kissing-gate where fine views open out ahead across and up the Colne valley towards Watford. Go through this, turn right and follow a right-hand fence downhill through two fields to a stile leading to a bridge over the M25. At the far end of the bridge bear half left across a large field with fine views ahead towards Maple Cross, Rickmansworth and Watford, heading for the left-hand end of a clump of bushes by Chalfont Road in the valley bottom. Turn right onto this road and follow it for half a mile into and through Maple Cross to reach your starting point.

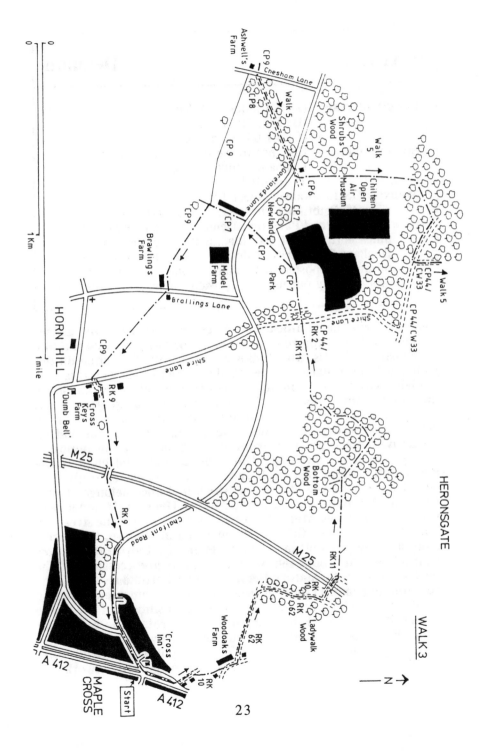

HERONSGATE

WALK 3

23

WALK 4   Denham

Length of Walk: (A) 5.5 miles / 8.8 Km
                      (B) 2.9 miles / 4.6 Km
                      (C) 4.1 miles / 6.5 Km
Starting Point: Entrance to the right-hand car park at
                      Denham Country Park.
Grid Ref: TQ049864
Maps: OS Landranger Sheet 176
            OS Pathfinder Sheet 1158 (TQ08/18)
How to get there / Parking: Denham Country Park, 1.5
  miles northwest of Uxbridge, may be reached from
  Denham Roundabout (M40 Junction 1) by taking a
  turning signposted to Denham Country Park for half a
  mile looking out for a signposted car park on your right.

Denham, near the confluence of the rivers Misbourne and Colne,
is today probably known best for its motorway junctions and to a
lesser extent, for its film studios and as a railway station on the
Chiltern Line. What many people do not realise, however, is that
hidden away from the major roads and the railway is one of the
most picturesque villages in the Chilterns. The village street, lined
with quaint red-brick, sometimes timber-framed sixteenth- to
eighteenth-century inns, shops and cottages, has at one end an
attractive village green in front of Denham Place, an imposing
mansion built for Sir Roger Hill in about 1688 and home in the
nineteenth century to Joseph and Lucien Bonaparte, brothers of
Napoleon, on the site of a house which had once belonged to Sir
Edmund Peckham, Master of the Mint to Henry VIII and a keen
supporter of Queen Mary. Towards the other end of the street are
Hill House, another fine seventeenth-century house, the parish
church, largely rebuilt in 1460 but retaining a fourteenth-century
chancel and thirteenth-century font from its predecessor, and the
partly seventeenth-century Denham Court Farmhouse. While the
surrounding countryside has been somewhat segmented by major
roads and modern development, the establishment of the Colne
Valley Regional Park has served both to protect the remaining
areas of unspoilt countryside and to improve public access to
them by creating a number of new footpaths and bridleways
which serve to link up the formerly rather disjointed network.

All three walks start from the Denham Country Park, visit or skirt the picturesque village and take advantage of some newly-created routes. Walks A and B additionally explore the Country Park with its pleasant riverside meadows and marshy woodlands rich in birdlife including herons and kingfishers and take in a section of the Grand Union Canal towpath with its unique atmosphere, while Walks A and C lead you to higher ground west of the village which offers fine views across the Colne Valley.

Walks A and B start from the entrance to the right-hand car park at Denham Country Park and turn right onto the road to the Rose Nursery. After 40 yards turn right through a kissing-gate onto path DN20, part of the South Bucks Way, disregarding a crossing bridle track and taking a gravel path straight on. Having passed through a further kissing-gate, follow a left-hand fence straight on across Misbourne Meadow. At the far side of the meadow go through a kissing-gate and ignore a path merging from your left. Some 30 yards further on, cross a bridge over the River Colne marking the old Middlesex county boundary. Now take path U52 straight on to reach the Grand Union Canal where the South Bucks Way ends.

Turn left onto the canal towpath (U75) and follow it for one third of a mile passing Denham Lock and Fran's Tea Garden to reach bridge no.182. Here turn left onto a raised unnumbered path then at a T-junction turn right onto a gravel bridle track and follow its winding course through a marshy tree-belt. After crossing a bridge, you skirt Flagmoor Meadow, which is being reclaimed as cow pasture to improve its wildlife value. At the far end of the meadow continue through more woodland ignoring a crossing path and crossing two small bridges where Denham Viaduct comes into view ahead. Erected in 1906 this viaduct formed part of the Great Central main line, the last major railway to be built into London before the proposed high-speed link to the Channel Tunnel. Here bear left crossing a bridge over an arm of the River Colne then bear right and follow an obvious winding path through Widows Cruise Covert, eventually crossing a large bridge over the main River Colne to reenter Buckinghamshire. Now take the fenced bridleway bearing right. On approaching another section of Denham Viaduct, at a fork go left and take a fenced bridleway through a belt of trees for a third of a mile with the railway embankment to your right and a golf course to your left. On leaving the tree-belt, go through a kissing-gate and turn left onto fenced macadam path DN17 joining the South Bucks Way. (NB There is access to or from Denham Station at this point via path DN17 and the station subway). Now take path DN17 for just over a quarter mile to the edge of Denham village where there is a kissing-gate to your left. Here **Walk A** continues on path DN17 to reach the village green by the gates of Denham Place, where you bear slightly left onto a bollarded path across the back of the green then turn right onto a roadside footway joining Walk C. Now omit the next two paragraphs.

Walk B turns left through the kissing-gate onto path DN19 rejoining the fenced bridle track. Where the bridle track bears left, take path DN19 straight on over a stile following a right-hand hedge then continuing across the churchyard to a gate and stile. Here turn right into a gravel lane. By Denham Church, where the lane becomes macadamed, turn left through ornamental gates then immediately right and follow a winding fenced bridle track for a quarter mile until you cross a bridge. Just after the bridge turn left through a kissing-gate onto path DN20 and follow a right-hand fence. Where the fenced bridle track bears away to the right, follow the bank of the Misbourne straight on across a fairway ignoring two bridges across the river then continue beside a left-hand tree-belt until you reach a kissing-gate in the right-hand fence. Now bear slightly right across the grass heading for gates ahead. Go through these and turn left for your starting point.

Walk C starts from the entrance to the right-hand car park at Denham Country Park and turns left along the road towards Denham Roundabout. After nearly 50 yards turn right through gates and head for the Colne Valley Park Centre. Here turn right along a gravel path to reach the fence of a golf course where you turn left onto path DN20, part of the South Bucks Way and go through a kissing-gate onto the golf course. Now turn left and take a worn path along the edge of the course until you reach a crossing macadam golfers´ path where the River Misbourne comes into view to your left. Here bear slightly left across a fairway to join a left-hand fence and follow it until you reach a kissing-gate. Go through this, turn right onto a fenced bridle track then immediately fork left through a handgate to a bend in Village Road, Denham where you go straight on. By Denham Church cross the road and continue along its left-hand footway through the village. Where the road forks by the village green, take the left-hand option crossing the road and taking its right-hand footway joining Walk A.

Walks A and C now continue over a footbridge beside a hump-backed bridge then briefly with one arm of the Misbourne to your left. At a road junction by the village hall ignore Cheapside Lane to your left and cross the road to use its left-hand footway. On reaching the A412, cross this busy road carefully. (If traffic is very

26

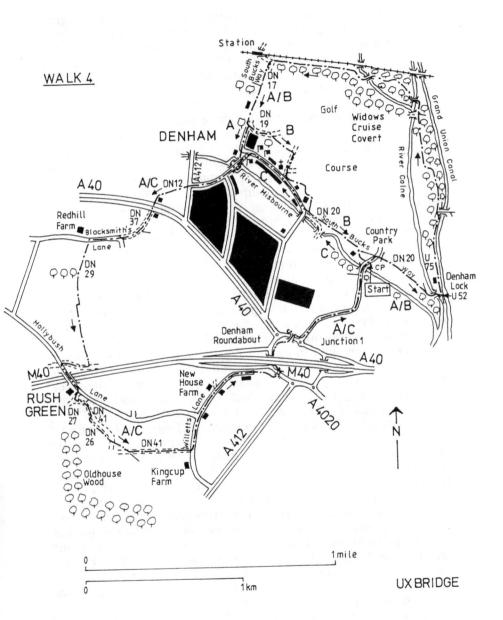

WALK 4

Station

South Bucks Way

DN 17

A/B

DN 19

DENHAM

A   B

Golf   Widows Cruise Covert

Course   River Colne

Grand Union Canal

A/C   DN12

A 40

River Misbourne

Redhill Farm

DN 37

Blacksmith's

Lane

DN 29

DN 20

South Bucks

B

Country Park

C

DN 20

Way

U 75

Start

A/B

Denham Lock

U 52

A 40

Hollybush

Denham Roundabout

A/C

Junction 1

A 40

M40

M40

A 4020

New House Farm

RUSH GREEN

DN 27

DN 41

Lane

Willetts Lane

A 412

N

DN 26

A/C

DN 41

Oldhouse Wood

Kingcup Farm

0   1 mile

0   1 km

UXBRIDGE

27

heavy, it may be preferable to turn left along it to the traffic lights at its junction with the A40, then cross the A40 and turn right along its far footway to rejoin the described route). Otherwise, at the far side of the A412 bear slightly left over a concealed stile onto path DN12 then bear slightly left across a field to a corner of a hedge. Here cross a stile and take a fenced path to the A40. Cross this busy dual-carriageway carefully and take path DN37 straight on along Blacksmith's Lane ignoring a branching path to your left. Having passed an overgrown gate, at a bend in a narrow lane go straight on. After some 230 yards at a slight right-hand bend turn left over a stile by a gate onto path DN29 with a fine view to your left towards Uxbridge. Now follow a right-hand fence and sporadic hedge over a rise into the next dip then cross a footbridge and stile and follow the right-hand hedge straight on uphill. At the top of the rise cross a stile in the hedge and continue along its other side through two fields to cross a stile near the M40. Now turn right onto a farm road beside the motorway to reach Hollybush Lane.

Turn left onto this road crossing the M40 bridge and passing an old farm at Rush Green now with views to your left up the Colne valley towards Denham and Harefield. Just past the old farmhouse turn right onto a rough track (path DN27). By a concreted gate-way, just before the track forks, turn left onto a grassy path across the green. At the far side of the green take bridleway DN41 straight on through gates with more views to your left towards Uxbridge and to your right towards Pinewood Film Studios. Where the fenced bridleway bears left, cross a stile by a gate in the right-hand hedge and turn left onto path DN26 beside a left-hand hedge to a stile. Cross this, the bridleway and another stile and bear slightly right across a field to a stile left of a clump of bushes. Now turn left rejoining fenced bridleway DN41 and following it for a quarter mile to a bridlegate into Willetts Lane. Turn left onto this quiet country road and follow it for nearly half a mile ignoring a branching road to your left and passing Rusholt House with its fine monkey-puzzle tree. On nearing the M40, the road narrows and then ends and you take a fenced macadam path straight on to reach Denham Roundabout. Here cross an elegant steel footbridge then take a macadam path straight on beside the inside of the round-about passing under the M40 flyover (beware - slippery bird-droppings!) and continuing to a further footbridge which you cross. At the far end turn sharp left under the bridge then at a small roundabout turn left onto the road to Denham Country Park and follow its walkable right-hand verge back to your starting point.

WALK 5   Chalfont St. Giles

Length of Walk: 5.2 miles / 8.5 Km
Starting Point: ´Crown`, Chalfont St. Giles.
Grid Ref: SU990935
Maps: OS Landranger Sheet 176
       OS Pathfinder Sheet 1139 (TQ09/19) & OS
       Explorer Sheet 3 (or old Pathfinder Sheet 1138
       (SU89/99))
       (Part only) Chiltern Society FP Map No.6
How to get there / Parking: Chalfont St. Giles, 3 miles
      southeast of Amersham, may be reached from the town
      by taking the A413 towards London to its junction with
      the B4442. Here turn right for the village centre where
      there is a signposted car park on the right.

Chalfont St. Giles, despite considerable modern expansion, can still boast a picturesque village centre with its small village green surrounded by attractive little shops, cottages and inns. The church, which is of twelfth-century origin but was remodelled in the fifteenth century, is reached from the green by means of an archway beneath part of a sixteenth-century cottage and is famous for its mediaeval wall paintings. The most notable building in the village, however, is Milton´s Cottage, where the poet took refuge from the plague in 1665. Built in about 1600, this cottage was where John Milton completed his ´Paradise Lost` and it was while he was staying here that Thomas Ellwood, who had secured the cottage for Milton, is said to have inspired Milton to write his ´Paradise Regained`.

The walk first leads you out of the village through meadows flanking the fitful River Misbourne before climbing to the quiet plateau separating it from the Colne valley to the east. Here you pass through Newland Park, where a short detour to visit the Chiltern Open Air Museum is well worthwhile, before circling through an extensive area of woodland on the Hertfordshire boundary to reach Nightingales Lane on the edge of the village. You now turn north and then descend into the Misbourne valley where a pleasant path leads you back into Chalfont St. Giles.

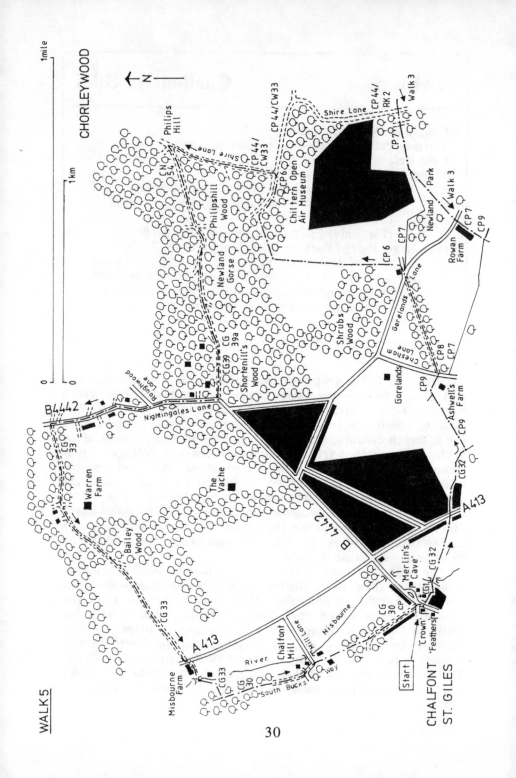

WALK 5

CHORLEYWOOD

30

Starting outside the 'Crown' in the centre of Chalfont St. Giles, cross the road and go through an archway opposite onto fenced path CG1 passing the churchyard to your left. Where the fenced path ends, ignore a stile to your right and take path CG32 straight on through a small gate and across a footbridge over the River Misbourne, which frequently dries up. Now take a worn path straight on across a meadow, with stepping stones over a stream at one point, to reach a kissing-gate. Here continue along a fenced path to cross the A413. Now take an enclosed path left of a gravel drive (still CG32) straight on uphill eventually with a paddock to your right. At the far end of this paddock fork left over a stile onto fenced path CP9 leading to another stile into a field. Cross this and follow a left-hand hedge at first. Where it bears left, go straight on across the field to a gap in a hedge left of a belt of trees. Now continue across the next field to cross two stiles in its far right-hand corner then turn right and follow a right-hand hedge to a gate and stile onto Chesham Lane. Here glance through a gate to your right for a view of Ashwell's Farm with its fine seventeenth-century timber-framed brick farmhouse and weather-boarded barn then bear slightly left across the road to pass through a gap by a gate onto bridleway CP8. Follow this through a belt of trees for a third of a mile to a road junction at the entrance to Newland Park.

The Chiltern Open Air Museum, which can be reached by taking the Park drive straight on, was conceived by the Chiltern Society as a project for European Architectural Heritage Year 1975 and was founded on County Council-owned land in Newland Park the following year. Opened to the public in 1981, the constantly-expanding museum consists largely of buildings of architectural interest which would otherwise have been lost through demolition but have instead been painstakingly taken down and rebuilt at Newland Park. It is open on Wednesday to Sunday and Bank Holiday afternoons from April to October.

The walk route crosses the major road (Gorelands Lane) and takes the Park drive, then just past the lodge bears half left onto path CP6 to cross a stile. Here bear slightly right across a parkland field to join the edge of Shrubs Wood and follow it, then a left-hand hedge with views towards the museum to your right. At the far side of the Park cross a stile into a wood called Newland Gorse bearing half right and following a left-hand fence downhill, later with a chestnut-paling fence to your right. Where the latter bears right, follow it for some 300 yards ignoring a crossing path and parallel path to your left until you reach a wide crossing bridleway at the edge of the wood.

Turn left onto this bridleway (CP44/CW33), known as Shire Lane because it straddles the Hertfordshire boundary, disregarding a branching permissive path to your left, and follow it up a sunken way ignoring another branching permissive path to the left. Near the top of Philips Hill turn left through a gap by a padlocked gate onto bridleway CN54 entering Philipshill Wood and following a wide track between plantations soon descending into a valley bottom. Here ignore a crossing permissive path and go straight on uphill soon entering mature woodland. The track, later bridleway CG39a, eventually becomes fenced and now as CG39, continues with houses and gardens to your right until you reach the B4442 (Nightingales Lane).

Turn right along its footway, which transfers to the left side of the road by the entrance to Shortenills Countryside Studies Centre and ends at the junction with Roughwood Lane. Now continue along the left-hand verge as far as it is walkable then cross the road and walk facing the oncoming traffic. After a third of a mile, by the entrance to 'Longacre' to your right, turn left crossing the road and taking path CG33 straight on along a rough tree-lined lane for half a mile eventually entering Bailey Wood. At the far side of the wood, where the main track bears left through a gate into a field and ends, take a fenced green lane straight on descending gently for over a third of a mile to reach the A413.

Cross this and go straight on down a macadam drive (still path CG33). By the entrance to a paper-recycling business go straight on across a footbridge over the River Misbourne then take a fenced path beside the river to cross a stile. Here turn right and follow a right-hand fence to cross a stile into a wood. Now turn left onto path CG30 joining the South Bucks Way and follow the inside edge of the wood. Where the trees eventually peter out, take a fenced track straight on to reach a bend in Mill Lane. Here go straight on along the road to a left-hand bend where a detour along the road to the left to the ford past the timber-framed millhouse of Chalfont Mill, reputedly the oldest watermill in the county, is well worthwhile. Otherwise leave the road at the bend and take a rough track (still path CG30) straight on. The track soon narrows to a path leading into a copse. In the copse follow a left-hand fence ignoring branching paths to your right and soon entering a wide avenue of chestnut and lime trees which then becomes a rough lane leading to the village street of Chalfont St. Giles near your starting point.

WALK 6   Coleshill (Hodgemoor Wood Picnic Area)

Length of Walk: 4.2 miles / 6.7 Km
Starting Point: Entrance to Hodgemoor Wood Picnic Area
Grid Ref: SU959942
Maps: OS Landranger Sheet 175
        OS Explorer Sheet 3 (or old Pathfinder Sheet 1138
        (SU89/99))
        Chiltern Society FP Maps Nos. 6 & 13
How to get there / Parking: Hodgemoor Wood Picnic Area,
    2 miles south of Amersham, may be reached from the
    town by taking the A355 towards Beaconsfield for 1.7
    miles and then turning left into a layby signposted
    'Picnic Area'. After 200 yards turn left again into
    Bottrells Lane looking out after 180 yards for the
    entrance to Hodgemoor Wood Picnic Area to your left.
    (NB The picnic area has barriers excluding vehicles taller
    than conventional cars. Such vehicles may be parked in
    the A355 layby).

Coleshill parish, in which your walk commences, was until **1832** a detached portion of Hertfordshire surrounded by Bucks. As such, in the seventeenth century it afforded a refuge to local Quakers who were persecuted by the authorities as they were safe here from the Buckinghamshire magistrates and when their Hertfordshire colleagues did make the long trip to Coleshill, the Quakers could quickly flee across the boundary into Bucks. One notable Quaker to live in Coleshill at this time was Thomas Ellwood, a friend of the poet John Milton, who lived for many years at Hunger Hill Farm (now Ongar Hill Farm) which you pass towards the end of your walk. The farm you see today, however, is not that of Thomas Ellwood as it was rebuilt in 1873.

    The walk, which is of an easy nature with plenty of woodland, quiet farmland and some pleasant views first leads you through Hodgemoor Wood to skirt the commuter village of Seer Green which has mushroomed from a tiny hamlet since the coming of the railway, then circles through a pleasant mixture of fields and woodland to reach Ongar Hill with its fine views to the north

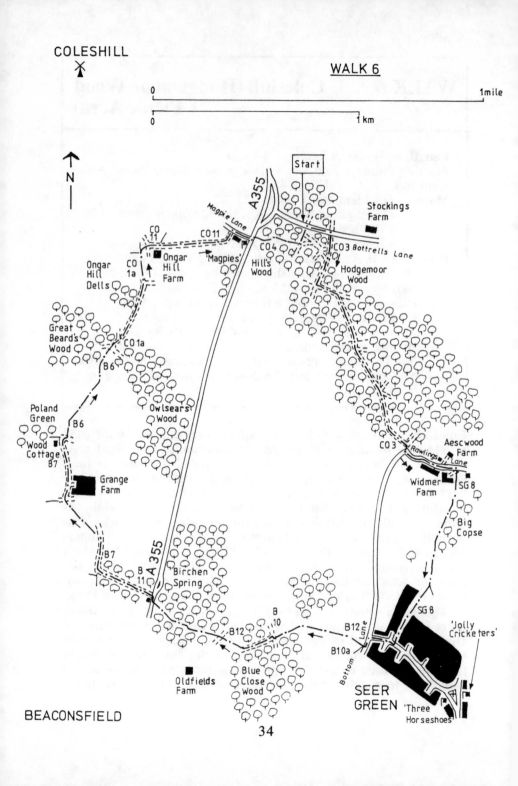

COLESHILL

WALK 6

0 ─────────────────────────── 1mile

0 ─────────────────────────── 1 km

N

Start

A355

Stockings Farm

Magpie Lane

CO 11

CO 11

CP

CO 3   Bottrells Lane

CO 4

'Magpies'

Hill's Wood

CO 3

Ongar Hill Dells

CO 1a

Ongar Hill Farm

Hodgemoor Wood

Great Beard's Wood

CO 1a

B 6

Poland Green

B 6

Owlsears Wood

Wood Cottage

B 7

Grange Farm

CO 3

Rawlings Lane

Aescwood Farm

Widmer Farm

SG 8

Big Copse

B 7

A 355

B 11

Birchen Spring

SG 8

B 10

'Jolly Cricketers'

B 12

B 12 Lane

B 10a

Bottom Lane

Oldfields Farm

Blue Close Wood

SEER GREEN

'Three Horseshoes'

BEACONSFIELD

34

before returning to your starting point.

Starting from the entrance to Hodgemoor Wood Picnic Area, turn left into Bottrells Lane. After about 130 yards turn right through a bollarded gap by a gate onto bridleway CO3 following the inside edge of the wood and ignoring all branching tracks and paths to your right. By the corner of a left-hand field bear left continuing to follow the inside edge of the wood. Just past a large pit to your right fork right leaving the edge of the wood and taking a wide bridleway disregarding all branching tracks or paths. On reaching the far side of the wood, the bridleway bears left and follows its inside edge for a short distance to a T-junction of tracks where you turn right passing a gate to reach a bend in Rawlings Lane.

Turn left onto this road and follow it for some 350 yards uphill at first then levelling out. Having passed Aescwood Farm to your left, just past a glass-fronted noticeboard turn right onto path SG8 crossing a concrete road and passing right of an old concrete garage to enter a fenced path. Follow this to a corner of Big Copse where you cross a stile and follow the outside edge of the wood then a left-hand hedge straight on through two fields. At the far side of the second field cross a stile and take a fenced path straight on for a quarter mile ignoring the stile of a branching path to your left then with back gardens to your right, later on both sides, until you come to a drive onto which you turn right to reach Orchard Road in Seer Green.

Turn right onto this road and follow it downhill ignoring side-turnings then at the bottom turn left into Bottom Lane. After about 50 yards turn right through a bridlegate onto bridleway B10a then cross a stile in front of you and take path B12 straight on uphill to an oak tree where you bear slightly left and head for a gap between two oak trees ahead. On reaching the corner of a hedge, cross a stile and follow a left-hand hedge then the outside edge of Blue Close Wood downhill to a stile into the wood. Inside the wood turn right onto crossing bridleway B10 then immediately turn left onto the continuation of path B12 following a track uphill through a mixed plantation. Just before reaching a gate with a ʻPrivate Woodlandˋ sign, turn right over a stile into a field then bear slightly right across the field passing just right of a small fenced sycamore tree to cross a stile into a wood called Birchen Spring. Here take an obvious path through this mixed plantation keeping right at a fork and continuing to a stile onto the A355.

Bear slightly right crossing this fast road carefully and take path B11 through lodge gates to follow a gravelly macadam drive along a fine avenue of trees. At the far end of the avenue follow the drive bearing right and joining path B7. After a further 200 yards fork left through a kissing-gate and cross a field diagonally to a stile by a small poplar at the near left-hand corner of Grange Farm. Cross this stile and bear slightly right across a concrete road to cross a stile by a gate and take a concrete road past a cowshed. Now bear slightly left through gates onto a fenced macadam farm road following a right-hand hedge to Wood Cottage. Here go through gates and ignore a branching path into a wood to your left called Poland Green. Now just round a sharp bend turn left onto fenced bridleway B6 beside a second left-hand gate and follow it downhill beside a left-hand hedge then the edge of Great Beard's Wood.

On entering the wood, ignore a crossing bridleway at the ancient county boundary and take bridleway CO1a following a woodland track straight on uphill. Disregard a branching track to your left then leave the wood and continue uphill along a sunken way passing a copse to your left known as Ongar Hill Dells then levelling out. At a field corner ignore a branching track to your right and bear slightly left through a hedge gap and across a field heading towards Coleshill Windmill to reach the corner of a hedge with fine views towards the stuccoed eighteenth-century Coleshill House on a hilltop to your right. Here turn right onto bridleway CO11 crossing a field to a stile into Ongar Hill Farm. Now bear half left joining a macadam drive and following it straight on, ignoring the stile of a branching path to your left and continuing soon on a rough track which becomes enclosed by hedges. Follow this downhill eventually bearing left to reach Magpie Lane. Turn right onto this road and follow it to the A355 by 'The Magpies'. Turn left onto this road then immediately turn right crossing the main road carefully and taking path CO4 over a culvert and stile into Hill's Wood. Follow this path uphill passing a deep chalkpit to your left and ignoring a branching path to your right. At a crossways by a tree with two trunks turn left onto a permissive path which leads to your starting point.

WALK 7   Penn

Length of Walk: (A) 5.4 miles / 8.8 Km
                           (B) 4.1 miles / 6.6 Km
Starting Point: Road junction by Penn Church.
Grid Ref: SU917933
Maps: OS Landranger Sheet 175
          OS Explorer Sheet 3 (or old Pathfinder Sheet 1138
(SU89/99))
          Chiltern Society FP Map No.13
How to get there / Parking: Penn, 3.2 miles east of the
    centre of High Wycombe, may be reached from the town
    by taking the A404 towards Amersham to Hazlemere.
    Here at the double mini-roundabout turn right onto the
    B474 towards Beaconsfield and follow it for 2.4 miles.
    Having passed Penn Church and the war memorial to
    your right and the ´Crown` to your left, pass a branching
    lane to your left and then park in a rough layby.
Notes: Bridleway P52 is prone to heavy nettle growth in the
    summer months and deep mud throughout the year.

Penn on a high ridge to the east of High Wycombe is potentially quite a vantage point as locals claim that between twelve and fifteen counties can be seen on a clear day from the church tower which was used in wartime as an air-raid wardens´ look-out post. At ground level, however, buildings and trees largely conceal these views but those who walk in the local countryside are soon rewarded with vistas largely unseen and unsuspected by those driving through the village on the B474. Despite its close proximity to High Wycombe, with which it is almost joined by continuous development, Penn, with its picturesque seventeenth-century inn and cottages clustered around its fine fourteenth-century church, has managed to preserve a remarkably rural atmosphere. Although it is relatively small in size, Penn also attracts visitors from across the Atlantic as the village gave its name to an important Bucks family, from whom William Penn, the leading Quaker and founder of Pennsylvania is said to descend and it is indeed after him that the state is now named.

    Both walks lead you southwards out of the village to Beacon Hill where fine views open out across the Wye valley. While

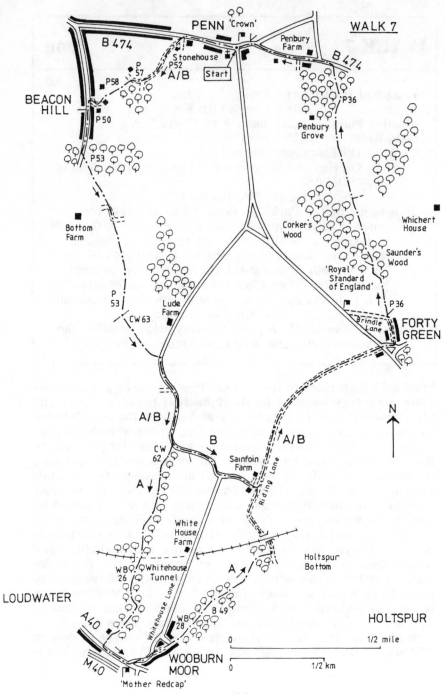

Walk A then continues down to Wooburn Moor before passing through a quiet valley near Holtspur, Walk B cuts off the corner to rejoin Walk A and climb gently to Forty Green, from which you proceed across a pleasant plateau with an alternation of woods and fields back into Penn.

Both walks start from the road junction by Penn Church and take the B474 westwards for some 300 yards. Just past ´Stonehouse`, which was regularly visited by King George III, by a walnut-tree and weatherboarded barn converted into garages, fork left onto enclosed bridleway P52 and follow it for nearly a quarter mile, soon narrowing and descending gently until you enter a wood. Here at a fork by an old pond bear right onto bridleway P57. Where it bears right, turn left over a stile onto path P58 and bear slightly right across a scrubby field to pass through a gap in the bushes left of a clump of hawthorn bushes then continue past an oak tree to cross a stile by a gate at the top edge of the field. Now continue between laurel hedges until you reach a gravel drive. Turn right onto this joining path P50 and passing right of Thae Cottage to reach a road at Beacon Hill.

Turn left onto this road and ignoring a branching path to your right, follow the road for 300 yards. Just past a house to your right called ´Claremont`, where the road narrows, turn left over a stile onto path P53 and bear half right across another scrubby field to a stile where fine views open out ahead towards Bottom Farm with its fine brick-and-timber farmhouse believed to be at least 500 years old and a weatherboarded barn and across the Wye valley towards the hilltop village of Flackwell Heath. Here bear slightly left across the field to a gate by the corner of a hedge. Do not go through this gate but bear slightly right through a hedge gap to join a fenced farm road and follow it straight on. Where the farm road bears left through a hedge gap, leave it and take the fenced path straight on beside a left-hand hedge, soon with vineyards to your right. On eventually crossing a stile, bear slightly right across a field to the corner of a hedge where you cross a stile by a gate and take path CW63 bearing slightly left and following a left-hand fence with fine views to your right across the Wye valley towards Flackwell Heath. Having passed a gate in the fence, bear left and follow a left-hand hedge to cross a stile by gates onto a road. Turn right and follow this road for a third of a mile with views to your left in places towards Holtspur until you reach a sharp left-hand bend.

Here Walk B continues along the road descending to a road junction where you fork left and continue downhill. Where the macadam road ends by the gates to Sainfoin Farm, take a rough lane straight on downhill to a T-junction of lanes where you turn left into Riding Lane rejoining Walk A. Now omit the next two paragraphs.

Walk A leaves the road at the left-hand bend and goes straight on over a stile onto fenced path CW62 entering a narrow belt of trees. Go straight on through this tree-belt for a third of a mile, soon with old orchards to your left and crossing two more stiles. Having crossed the second stile, you enter a copse concealing the mouth of Whitehouse Tunnel to your right and take path WB26 passing through the copse then continuing through a tree-belt, starting to descend, bearing left then right and eventually reaching the A40 at Wooburn Moor in the Wye valley on the edge of the industrial suburb of Loudwater.

Turn left onto its footway then opposite the ´Mother Redcap` turn left into Whitehouse Lane. At the second left-hand bend fork right onto path WB28 following the drive to ´Cornwall Cottage` ignoring branching drives to left and right. By ´Cornwall Cottage` leave the drive and take a fenced path straight on, soon crossing the end of a residential cul-de-sac and continuing until you reach rails into a hillside copse. Climb through these and keep straight on through the copse (soon on path B49) eventually emerging over a stile with views up Holtspur Bottom ahead towards the edge of Holtspur and Beaconsfield. Here take the fenced path straight on beside a left-hand hedge. At the far side of the field cross a stile and bear right following the fenced path beside a right-hand hedge downhill, ignoring gates to right and left, to reach a stile into Riding Lane near the foot of a high railway embankment. Turn left onto this unmade county road passing under a high railway arch and continuing for some 350 yards to a junction of lanes by Sainfoin Farm where you go straight on rejoining Walk B.

Walks A and B now take Riding Lane straight on for two-thirds of a mile following the valley bottom at first then climbing over a ridge and dropping to a road junction at Forty Green near the sixteenth-century brick-and-timber Hill Farm Cottage with its weatherboarded barn. Some 300 yards to your left is the ´Royal Standard of England`, an ancient hostelry formerly known as ´The Ship Inn`, which is believed to have been renamed thus in the late seventeenth century to mark its use as a refuge and temporary headquarters by King Charles I during the Civil War. If not visiting this inn, bear half right onto the priority road and follow it uphill. Just before a left-hand bend turn left into Brindle Lane and follow this gravel road uphill. At the top, where the gravel road turns left, leave it and take path P36 straight on over a stile by padlocked gates and across a field to cross a stile by gates. Here bear slightly left across a second field to cross two stiles and enter Saunder's Wood. Inside the wood bear left then at a waymarked fork take the right-hand option straight on, soon leaving the wood again. Now follow its outside edge, then a hedge, then the outside edge of Penbury Grove straight on through five fields and an area of scrub with views to your right across a valley towards some large modern houses at Knotty Green. On crossing a stile into the wood, follow a left-hand fence straight on through it to a stile onto the B474. Cross this busy road carefully and turn left along its narrow but mostly walkable far verge. Now follow it ignoring branching roads to your right and branching paths to your left and passing Penbury Farm, after which William Penn named his house in America, to reach your starting point.

WALK 8   Hughenden

Length of Walk: 4.6 miles / 7.4 Km
Starting Point: Hughenden Church car park.
Grid Ref: SU865955
Maps: OS Landranger Sheets 165 & 175
       OS Explorer Sheet 3 (or old Pathfinder Sheet 1138 (SU89/99))
       Chiltern Society FP Map No.12
How to get there / Parking: Hughenden Church, 1.5 miles north of High Wycombe, may be reached from the town by taking the A4128 towards Great Missenden for 1.5 miles and turning left onto a side road signposted to Hughenden Manor. Cross a cattle grid then take a left fork to a parking area in front of the church.
Notes: Heavy nettle growth may be encountered on path D6 in summer.

Hughenden, formerly ´Hitchenden `, is the name of a parish, its church and its manor house, but no ancient village of this name exists. The church and nearby manor house both have close links with the Victorian prime minister, Benjamin Disraeli, 1st Earl of Beaconsfield, who owned Hughenden Manor from 1848 till his death in 1881. He entertained Queen Victoria here in 1877 and extensively remodelled the eighteenth-century house, the park and the thirteenth-century church according to his own eccentric taste. He is buried in the churchyard and a plaque in his memory was erected near his accustomed pew by Queen Victoria in 1882.

The walk with its alternation of fine views and characteristic Chiltern beechwoods leads you uphill through woodland to the Naphill plateau and across fields to Hunt´s Hill and Naphill´s wooded common. You then continue with fine views to Downley´s open common before going through the village and more woodland to Tinker´s Hill and the Disraeli Monument. From here you drop through a wood and a housing estate into Hughenden Park, through which you return to your starting point.

Starting from the back of Hughenden church car park go through gates into the churchyard and take a macadam path passing left of the church to a gate by Church House into Hughenden Park. Now take path H51 straight on uphill. On nearing a gate, turn right by a hawthorn bush onto path H13 crossing the drive to Hughenden Manor, going through a gate and taking a fenced concrete path. By a cottage gate leave the concrete path and go straight on, soon bearing left and climbing through woodland. Where a fine view across Hughenden Valley towards Cryers Hill opens out to your right, disregard a crossing permissive path with a stile and continue, soon entering Woodcock Wood. Here ignore a crossing path then go through a kissing-gate into the corner of a field. Now follow the left-hand fence straight on along the edge of Hanging Wood to a stile. Cross this then turn right through a kissing-gate onto a fenced grassy track and follow it for 250 yards. Where the track bears right, turn left over a stile onto path H14 bearing half right across a field to the right-hand corner of Flagmore Wood. Here ignore a stile into the wood and follow its outside edge straight on through two fields. In the second field disregard a branching path to your right and another stile into the wood then continue beside a left-hand hedge to a stile in the field corner. Now take a fenced path straight on to a stile into Hunt's Hill Lane on the edge of Naphill.

Turn left onto this road. After a quarter mile, where its surface ends, turn right onto a stony track along the edge of Naphill Common bearing left by a green gate and later left again across the common. Before reaching the far side of the common, turn left between bollards onto crossing bridleway D20. Ignore a branching path to your left and after 100 yards turn right onto waymarked path D6. Now cross a stile and bear slightly left across a field, heading just right of a gap in the trees in Little Cookshall Wood through which West Wycombe's hilltop church with its golden ball can be seen ahead, to cross a stile into the wood. Keep straight on through the wood soon joining the squirrel-fence of a left-hand plantation. After some 300 yards, soon after this fence turns left, turn left onto crossing path D5 and follow it uphill soon rejoining the squirrel-fence. On leaving the wood, follow a left-hand hedge straight on over a hilltop with superb views opening out to your right towards West Wycombe Church and the hilltop village of Lane End beyond and later ahead over Downley towards Cressex. At the far end of the field go through a kissing-gate then straight on across the next field passing just right of a brick-and-flint cottage to a gate and kissing-gate into Plomer Green Lane at Downley Common.

Turn left onto this road, soon bearing right. At the end of the road turn right onto a stony track (path D4) and follow it downhill. Where the track bears left by a wooden lamppost, bear slightly right between bollards ignoring two crossing paths and heading for a crabtree. Now bear slightly right and aim left of a flint cottage soon passing between bollards and taking a flinty track downhill to the end of a road called Moor Lane. A few yards along this road, by the entrance to a pumping station, turn left onto the right-hand of two branching paths (D12), bearing half left uphill. At a fork keep left then ignore a path merging from your left and continue uphill across the common to a road junction at Downley.

Here cross the major road known as Common Side and take Narrow Lane straight on downhill to a T-junction. Now cross Littleworth Road bearing slightly left into a wide macadam drive. At the far end of the drive bear half right onto path D11 towards a wire-mesh fence then pass through a concealed kissing-gate and take a fenced path downhill into Little Tinker's Wood. In the wood fork left onto path HW136 and go straight on for a quarter mile disregarding all branching or crossing paths to reach a fork near the far side of the wood. Here bear left then ignore a branching path to the left and leave the wood at Tinker's Hill by the Disraeli Monument, built in 1862 in memory of Disraeli's father, Isaac, the antiquary and writer who lived at Bradenham Manor from 1829 till his death in 1848. Here there are fine views across the Hughenden valley with Hughenden Manor on a hilltop to your left.

Follow the fence past the monument into Great Tinker's Wood, then bear half right ignoring a branching path to your left. At a three-way fork take the middle option downhill. Near the bottom of the dip fork left onto path HW137 bearing left and ignoring branching paths to your right. On leaving the wood, go down an alleyway to Wyndham Avenue. Here turn right then at a T-junction turn left into Disraeli Crescent downhill to a T-junction with Coates Lane. Cross this road bearing slightly right through bollards onto a permissive route through parkland. (If closed, an alternative route via Coates Lane and path HW28 is shown on the plan). Ignore a stile to your right and follow a playground fence to a gap in the next hedge into Hughenden Park then bear slightly right down a line of lime trees towards a bridge over Hughenden Brook. On reaching a newly-planted crossing avenue of trees, turn left into it joining path HW28. Having passed two large oak trees, leave the avenue and bear slightly right keeping left of the brook to cross a stile by a red waste bin into National Trust land where the car park comes into view ahead. Here bear slightly right along a worn permissive path towards the car park crossing a stile by a gate and continuing to your starting point. (If this permissive route is closed, an alternative via paths H13 and H51 is shown on the plan).

44

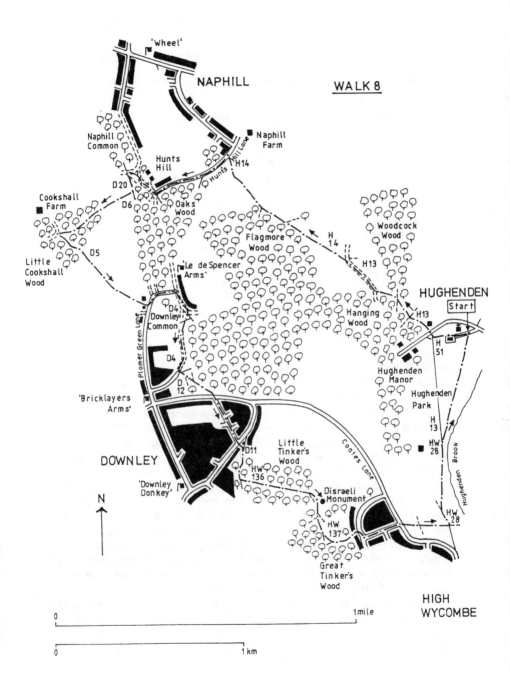

WALK 8

'Wheel'

NAPHILL

Naphill
Common

Naphill
Farm

Hunts
Hill

Hunts

Mill Lane

H14

D20

Cookshall
Farm

D6

Oaks
Wood

Woodcock
Wood

Flagmore
Wood

H
14

Little
Cookshall
Wood

D5

'Le de Spencer
Arms'

H13

HUGHENDEN

Start

Hanging
Wood

H13

D4
Downley
Common

Plomer Green Lane

H
51

D4

Hughenden
Manor

'Bricklayers
Arms'

D
12

Hughenden
Park

H
13

D11

Little
Tinker's
Wood

HW
28

DOWNLEY

HW
136

Coates Lane

'Downley
Donkey'

Disraeli
Monument

Hughenden Brook

N

HW
28

HW
137

Great
Tinker's
Wood

HIGH
WYCOMBE

0   1mile

0   1 km

45

WALK 9   West Wycombe

Length of Walk: 4.8 miles / 7.8 Km
Starting Point: Entrance to car park in Chorley Road, West
           Wycombe.
Grid Ref: SU827947
Maps: OS Landranger Sheets 165 & 175
       OS Explorer Sheet 3 (or old Pathfinder Sheet 1138
       (SU89/99))
       Chiltern Society FP Map No.7
How to get there / Parking: West Wycombe, 2.5 miles north-
     west of the centre of High Wycombe, may be reached
     from the town by taking the A40 towards Oxford. Having
     passed through West Wycombe village, fork right into
     Chorley Road (variously signposted to Bledlow Ridge or
     Bledlow) where the car park is on the left after 150 yards.
Notes: Path PW23 is prone to heavy nettle growth in the
     summer months.

West Wycombe, though separated by only 300 yards of open countryside from the edge of High Wycombe, has succeeded in retaining its village atmosphere thanks to the Royal Society of Arts who bought it from the Dashwood Estate in 1929 and subsequently gave it to the National Trust to preserve in 1934. The High Street, though somewhat marred by the incessant traffic which funnels through it, is flanked by a superb array of picturesque mainly sixteenth- to eighteenth-century cottages, shops and inns but is crowned by Church Loft with its jutting upper storey dating from 1417. On the hill above it within an Iron Age hill fort is St. Lawrence's Church renowned for the golden ball on the top of its tower. Originally built in the thirteenth century to serve the lost hilltop village of Haveringdon, it was extensively rebuilt in 1763 by Sir Francis Dashwood, Lord le Despencer, with its nave remodelled to resemble the Temple of the Sun at Palmyra and its tower heightened and capped with the golden ball, in which at least six people could sit, copied from the Customs Building in Venice. Next to the church he also built a family mausoleum based on Constantine's Arch in Rome. Below the church are the Hellfire Caves dug in about 1750 to provide flints for the realigned turnpike road to High Wycombe. Legend has it that Dashwood and his Hellfire Club held orgies in the caves although this is thought to have resulted from slurs by Dashwood's political opponents at a time when he was Chancellor of the Exchequer. On the other side of the village is the early eighteenth-century West Wycombe Park which Dashwood also remodelled in the Palladian style with colonnades, classical porticos and a luxurious interior decor and grounds laid out by Humphrey Repton.

The walk, characterised by an alternation of pleasant woodland and superb views across the hills, first skirts the village and offers views of West Wycombe Park before climbing to the hilltop hamlet of Towerage. You then pass through woods and descend to the edge of Piddington before climbing again to the edge of the scattered village of Radnage, from which you return by way of a quiet Chiltern bottom and a disused ancient roadway.

Starting from the entrance to the car park, turn right into Chorley Road. At its junction with the A40 turn right onto it then after some 200 yards turn left into Toweridge Lane. Take this road uphill for nearly half a mile looking out for two gateways on your left giving views of the west and south façades of West Wycombe House and fine views to your right up the valley towards Myze Farm and Piddington then continuing through High Wood to the end of the macadam road on the edge of the scattered hamlet of Towerage.

Here fork right onto bridleway WW24 and take this flint lane ignoring a track merging from the left. Where the lane forks and the main track turns left towards Towerage Farm, fork right through a gateway and take bridleway HW130 straight on along a grassy track by a right-hand hedge passing a pylon. At a further fork by a wooden pylon keep right entering Hellbottom Wood. Just past a telecommunication tower turn right onto path HW135a soon entering a field where there is a fine view to your right towards St. Lawrence's Church on its hilltop. Take path WW25 bearing slightly right across the field to a gap in the edge of Upper Dorrels Wood. Go through this and take path HW135 following a winding track through the wood. At the far side of the wood, where the track forks, go left and then right to cross a stile then take path PW13 beside a left-hand hedge. Where the hedge ends, follow the outside edge of a copse called Sheepskin's Shaw straight on looking out for a stile into the copse. Cross this and take the obvious path to reach Bullocks Lane.

Turn left onto this road ignoring a bridleway to your left.

Opposite Bullocks Farm fork right onto path PW12 taking a flint track into Jane's Wood. After 50 yards turn right over a stile onto path PW14 descending through a mature plantation. On entering a new plantation where there are fine views to your right towards West Wycombe and to your left across Piddington, the path swings to the left and follows the contours of the hillside but continues to descend gradually. Eventually you ignore a branching path to your left and cross a stile at the bottom edge of the plantation. Now go straight downhill to cross a stile by a gate left of Lower Farm leading to Old Oxford Road, the original line of the A40, on the edge of Piddington, a new industrial settlement created in 1903 when Sir George Dashwood forced North's expanding furniture factory to move out of West Wycombe.

Turn left onto this road and follow it past this hillside village. Having passed the former furniture factory whose tall chimney has now been demolished, at a road junction by the 'Dashwood Arms' cross the A40 and take bridleway PW27, the central of three rough tracks, towards the eighteenth-century Ham Farm. By some weatherboarded barns fork left through double gates and a bridle-gate onto a fenced track beside a right-hand hedge. Having joined a larger track, after some 200 yards turn right through a small hurdle-gate onto path PW26 following a left-hand fence steeply uphill to cross a stile into a wood where there is a fine view behind you across Ham Farm towards Piddington and Wheeler End on a hilltop to the right. Now follow the left-hand fence uphill through the wood to cross a stile into a field. Here turn left along the edge of the wood to cross a stile in a corner of the field where a fine view opens out ahead up Plomer's Bottom towards Radnage and the BT tower near Stokenchurch. Now bear half right up the field heading for the right-hand end of a tall hedge. Here do **not** cross the stile but turn left following a right-hand hedge. In a corner of the field cross a rail-stile by a gate and take path RA27 following a left-hand hedge, later joining a rough track and continuing to a bend in the road at Green End on the edge of Radnage.

Here turn right into Hatch Lane. After some 30 yards turn right again onto path RA28 bearing half left off the farm track through a fence gap and crossing a field diagonally to enter Chawley Wood in the bottom corner of the field. Now at a T-junction of paths turn right onto path PW23 following the bottom edge of the wood for some 300 yards to cross a stile into a field where a fine view opens out to your right towards St. Lawrence's Church on its hilltop. Bear half right across the field to cross a concealed stile at the right-hand end of a tall hedge then bear half right across the next field

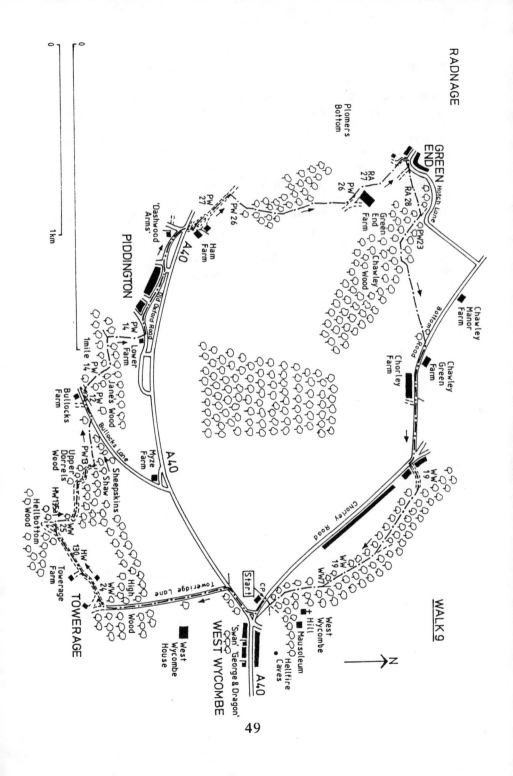

49

heading for a bungalow with tall chimneys surrounded by trees to pass through an old gateway and continue to Bottom Road, part of the ancient road from London to Oxford and South Wales. Turn right onto this passing Chawley Green Farm to your left with its timber-framed seventeenth-century farmhouse and Chorley Farm to your right with another timber-framed seventeenth-century farmhouse and a timbered barn to reach a crossroads at the farthest extent of Wycombe's pre-war ribbon development which threatened to envelop the Chilterns before the Second World War and modern planning controls put a stop to it. Turn right into Chorley Road then immediately left onto path WW19, a rough lane which formed the continuation of the ancient London road, soon climbing into scrubby woodland then narrowing and levelling off to follow the contours of the hillside with views to your right across the valley in places. Ignore a path merging from your left then eventually, by an anti-horse barrier, bear slightly right onto path WW7 descending gently. At a fork ignore a branching path to your left then, on emerging onto the open hillside, turn right onto a permissive path downhill to the car park.

WALK 10   Chinnor Hill

Length of Walk: 5.0 miles / 8.0 Km
Starting Point: Chinnor Hill car park.
Grid Ref: SP766002
Maps: OS Landranger Sheet 165
        OS Explorer Sheets 2 & 3 (or old Pathfinder Sheets
        1117 (SP60/70) & 1137 (SU69/79))
        Chiltern Society FP Maps Nos. 7 & 14
How to get there / Parking: Chinnor Hill, 7.5 miles north-
    west of High Wycombe, may be reached from the town
    by taking the A40 towards Oxford for 2.5 miles. Having
    passed through West Wycombe, fork right onto the
    Bledlow Ridge road and follow it for 5.3 miles through
    Bledlow Ridge and continuing to a sharp left-hand bend
    with woodland to your right. Here turn right into Hill
    Top Lane and follow it to a rough car park at its far end.
Notes: Heavy nettle growth may be encountered at several
    points in the summer months.

Chinnor Hill with its extensive views across Oxfordshire and the
Vale of Aylesbury has always been a popular destination for
picnickers, walkers and motorists. Since it became a nature
reserve, the Berkshire, Buckinghamshire & Oxfordshire
Naturalists´ Trust (BBONT) has endeavoured to control the
scrub which was rapidly invading the chalk downland in order to
preserve its flora including rare orchids and the fine views which
might easily have been obscured. When sitting on this hilltop on a
quiet sunny afternoon, it is, however, hard to imagine that what is
now a sunken bridleway through the scrub below you was on
18th June 1643 the scene of a bloody skirmish when Prince
Rupert and his Royalist troops ambushed a Roundhead regiment
transporting £21,000 from their headquarters in Thame to
London and subsequently set light to the village of Chinnor to
prevent its use as a base by enemy forces.

   The walk, which offers a wealth of fine views both out onto the
plain and across the hills, leads you first along the ridge towards
Bledlow Ridge to the hamlet of Rout´s Green before descending
into a quiet hollow at Callow Down. You then circle round the
foot of Wain Hill with its steep wooded slopes and bronze age

51

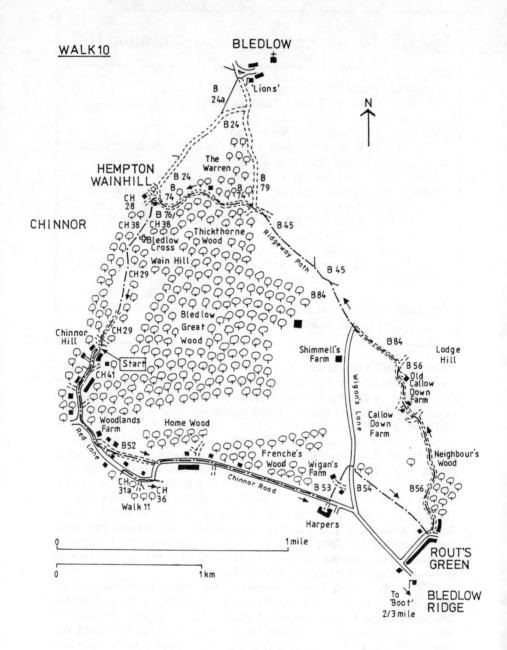

WALK 10

BLEDLOW

'Lions'

B 24a

B 24

The Warren

N

HEMPTON
WAINHILL

B 24

B 79

B 74

B 74

CH 28

B 76

B 45

CHINNOR

CH 38 CH 38

Bledlow Cross

Thickthorne Wood

Ridgeway Path

B 45

Wain Hill

CH 29

B 84

Bledlow Great Wood

Chinnor Hill

CH 29

Start

CH 41

Shimmell's Farm

B 84

Lodge Hill

B 56
Old Callow Down Farm

Wigan's Lane

Callow Down Farm

Neighbour's Wood

Woodlands Farm

Home Wood

Red Lane

B 52

Frenche's Wood

Wigan's Farm

B 53

B 54

B 56

CH 31a

CH 36

Chinnor Road

Walk 11

Harpers

ROUT'S GREEN

0   1 mile

0   1 km

To 'Boot' 2/3 mile

BLEDLOW RIDGE

52

barrow before climbing a sunken way to cross the top of Chinnor Hill and return to your starting point.

Starting from the car park at Chinnor Hill, walk southwards along Hill Top Lane (CH41) to the T-junction. Here turn left into Red Lane then some 50 yards past a bus stop, by the entrance to Woodlands Farm, fork left over a concealed stile onto path B52 following a left-hand hedge then a fence over several stiles to reach a farmyard. Now take a concrete road then a grassy track straight on to gates and a stile leading to a bend in Chinnor Road. Take this road straight on for three-quarters of a mile with a fine view to your left at one point towards Princes Risborough and Whiteleaf Cross, a chalk cross carved into the hillside of unknown origin. On nearing a road junction, just past the entrance to Harpers to your right, turn left over a stile onto path B53 and follow a left-hand hedge to Wigan´s Farm. Here cross two stiles and go straight on downhill to cross a stile in the bottom corner of the field. Now go through a belt of scrub, cross another stile and descend some steps into Wigan´s Lane opposite the entrance to a former council tip.

Cross the road and take path B54 bearing right between hedges into a field. Here bear left and follow the left-hand hedge through two fields, later with fine views to your left over Lodge Hill, where neolithic tools and bronze age burial mounds and pottery have been found, towards Whiteleaf Cross and the hillside village of Loosley Row and hilltop village of Lacey Green with its seventeenth-century windmill. Soon after the hedge peters out, cross a stile and follow a right-hand fence straight on through a paddock to cross another stile. Now continue along a fenced path to a road at the hamlet of Rout´s Green.

Turn left onto this road and, disregarding a fork to your right, follow it to the end of its macadam surface. Here bear left and take bridleway B56, a rough lane which soon narrows and enters Neighbour´s Wood. Ignore a hedge gap to your left and bear half right following the inside edge of the wood downhill, soon in a sunken way. On leaving the wood, continue along a green lane. Where its right-hand hedge ends, more fine views open out to your right towards Lodge Hill, Loosley Row and Lacey Green. On reaching a crossing track, go straight on into a green lane, soon emerging at Callow Down Farm. Here take a concrete track straight on between the farmhouse and the farm buildings then bear slightly right into another green lane which soon passes Old Callow Down Farm with its early seventeenth-century half-timbered farmhouse and attractive cottage garden. By the farm buildings

53

join a farm road and follow it straight on. Where it bears left, continue to follow it, now on path B84 and with fine views to your right towards Princes Risborough and Whiteleaf Cross, until you reach Wigan's Lane.

Cross this road and a stile opposite and bear half right across a field to cross a stile in its far corner onto the Ridgeway Path (B45) where there are superb views towards the Ashendon Hills to your left, Aylesbury, Princes Risborough and Whiteleaf Cross ahead and Lacey Green, Loosley Row and Lodge Hill to your right. Here turn left onto path B45 soon passing through a kissing-gate then following a right-hand fence with more fine views to your right in places and ignoring a stile of a branching path to your right. On reaching the bottom of a dip where the fence bears away to your right, leave it and go straight on to a kissing-gate just right of the far corner of the field and a corner of Thickthorne Wood. Go through this and turn left onto the Upper Icknield Way (byway B74) ignoring a branching bridleway to your right and entering the wood. Now follow a terraced track around the contours of the steep north face of Wain Hill with glimpses through the trees to your right of Bledlow with its thirteenth-century church.

After half a mile by a large red-brick cottage and former inn known as the 'Leather Bottle' straddling the Bucks/Oxon boundary at Hempton Wainhill (pronounced and formerly spelt 'Wynnal') turn left onto bridleway CH28 then just past the cottage fork left again onto bridleway B76/CH38 leaving the Ridgeway Path and Upper Icknield Way, climbing the face of Wain Hill and soon entering a sunken way. Ignoring a raised path on its right-hand bank, take this sunken way (now CH38) uphill passing below Bledlow Cross, another chalk hillside landmark of unknown origin and eventually emerging onto a terraced path near the top of the hill. Here ignore a branching path to the left, go past the BBONT noticeboard, enter some scrub and disregard a branching path to your right. Now on bridleway CH29, on reaching the open hilltop, there is a seat some 20 yards to your right with fine views across Chinnor towards Didcot Power Station and the Downs to your left and Oxford and the Ashendon Hills ahead. Now rejoin bridleway CH29 and follow it across the hilltop into more woodland through which you continue in order to reach your starting point.

Length of Walk: 5.5 miles / 8.9 Km
Starting Point: Stokenchurch Post Office.
Grid Ref: SU760963
Maps: OS Landranger Sheet 165
OS Explorer Sheet 3 (or old Pathfinder Sheet 1137 (SU69/79)
Chiltern Society FP Map No.14
How to get there / Parking: Stokenchurch, 7 miles west of High Wycombe, may be reached by leaving the M40 at Junction 5 (Stokenchurch) and taking the A40 into the centre of the village. There is a free public car park outside the 'King's Arms Hotel'.
Notes: Heavy nettle growth may be encountered at several points in the summer months.

Stokenchurch on the London-Oxford road on a ridgetop plateau about a mile from the escarpment and one of the highest major settlements in the Chilterns has the unfortunate reputation of being 'the ugly duckling' of the Chilterns. This may arise from its former role as a centre of the Bucks furniture industry with its factories and timber yards or from the extent to which it has been developed for housing since the coming of the M40. Nevertheless the village, only transferred from Oxfordshire to Bucks in 1896, can boast extensive, attractive, well-maintained village greens where an annual horse fair used to be held on July 10th and 11th and a funfair is held to this day. The twelfth-century parish church hidden behind the 'King's Arms ' is quite sizeable when one considers that until 1844 it was merely a chapel-of-ease for Aston Rowant and despite many renovations it is still worth a visit. This is also the burial place of Hannah Ball (1734-1792), a friend of John Wesley who founded the first English Sunday school in High Wycombe in 1769. For the walker, however, the chief attraction of Stokenchurch is that it is an ideal centre for exploring some of the finest Chiltern countryside including the Wormsley Valley, Penley Bottom, Radnage and the escarpment.

This walk explores the quiet country of high ridges and deep bottoms to the northeast of Stokenchurch crossing the county boundary no less than six times and offers a mixture of Chiltern

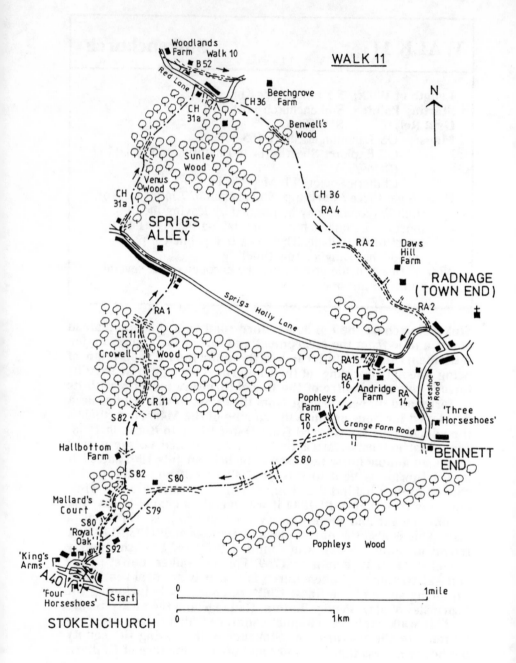

WALK 11

Woodlands Farm Walk 10
B 52
Red Lane
CH 36
Beechgrove Farm
CH 31a
CH
Benwell's Wood
Sunley Wood
Venus Wood
CH 31a
CH 36
RA 4
SPRIG'S ALLEY
RA 2
Daws Hill Farm
RADNAGE (TOWN END)
RA 1
Sprigs Holly Lane
RA 2
CR11
Crowell Wood
RA15
RA 16
Andridge Farm
RA 14
Horseshoe Road
'Three Horseshoes'
CR 11
Pophleys Farm
CR 10
S 82
Grange Farm Road
Hallbottom Farm
BENNETT END
S 82
S 80
S 80
Mallard's Court
S 79
'Royal Oak'
S 80
S 92
Pophleys Wood
'King's Arms'
A 40
'Four Horseshoes'
Start

STOKENCHURCH

N

0 ———————————— 1mile
0 ———————————— 1km

beechwoods and superb views, first heading north over several ridges to reach Red Lane before descending into Radnage Bottom and returning by way of Andridge to Stokenchurch.

Starting from Stokenchurch Post Office opposite the ´King´s Arms`, cross the A40 and follow the left-hand edge of a green straight on to a road. Turn left onto this and at a five-way junction by the ´Royal Oak` turn right into Park Lane. Where the macadam road turns left to Longburrow Hall, take a rough road (path S92, later S80) straight on for a third of a mile ignoring a branching path to your right and several drives and a path to your left. Having passed through a belt of woodland, where a fine view opens out ahead across Hall Bottom towards Andridge Farm and Bledlow Ridge and the road forks, bear left onto path S82 taking a tarmac drive downhill. Where the drive bears left into the wood, fork right over a stile and descend steeply to cross a stile in the bottom right-hand corner of the paddock. Now bear left following a left-hand hedge downhill. At the bottom corner of the field go straight on through a hedge gap then bear slightly right across the next field to cross a concealed stile in its top hedge. Now bear half right across a further field to a fence gap with a stile step leading into Crowell Wood.

In the wood ignore a crossing bridleway called Colliers Lane, an ancient road from London to Oxford and South Wales once used to transport coal to London. Now in Oxfordshire, take path CR11 steeply uphill through this wood devastated by a hurricane in 1990 when 54 fallen trees blocked the path! At the top of the hill, on entering mature beechwoods, take the waymarked path straight on ignoring a crossing track and dropping into the next valley. Here disregard a crossing bridleway and back in Bucks take path RA1 straight on over a stile then bear slightly right up a field to a stile in its top hedge. Now keep straight on beside a left-hand fence to a farm. Here join the drive and follow it to Sprig´s Holly Lane.

The hamlet of Sprig´s Holly (Bucks) or Sprig´s Alley (Oxon) is scattered along a mile of ridgetop road. Some people believe the variation in its name results from attempts to refine the word ´Alley`, while others think that it comes from local people dropping their Hs, but old maps suggest the first explanation to be correct!

Turn left onto this road and follow it for a quarter mile reenter-ing Oxfordshire and passing the ´Sir Charles Napier Restaurant`. At a left-hand bend opposite a pair of white cottages turn right onto bridleway CH31a taking the centre of three tracks along the edge of a tree belt. Where the tree belt widens into Venus Wood, bear slightly left through a bridlegate and follow the generally enclosed narrow bridleway down the edge of the wood. At the bottom go through a bridlegate, ignore a bridleway to your right and continue uphill through Sunley Wood, later joining a right-hand fence and following it to Red Lane near Sunley Farm. Turn right onto this road passing a weatherboarded former pub called ˊThe Pheasantˋ and ignoring a bridleway to your right. At a sharp left-hand bend turn right over a stile by a gate onto path CH36 following a left-hand hedge to a gate and stile into Benwellˊs Wood. At the far side of the wood where a fine view opens out ahead towards Radnage City and a distant hill near Lane End, follow the left-hand hedge downhill to cross a stile at the county boundary. Now take path RA4 bearing half left across a field to cross a stile by a gate in its far left-hand corner. Here take bridleway RA2 straight on along a narrow green lane, later joining a macadam drive and continuing along it to a road at the edge of Radnage Town End.

Here turn right into Sprigˊs Holly Lane and follow it steeply uphill. At the top turn left onto path RA15, the drive to Andridge Farm. Where the drive bears left, turn right over two stiles onto path RA16 then turn left beside a left-hand hedge. On crossing another stile, turn left through a hedge gap where fine views open out up Hall Bottom towards Stokenchurch. Now follow the left-hand hedge downhill. By an electricity pole to your left, bear half right across the field to its bottom corner. Here go through a hedge gap, cross Grange Farm Road and the county boundary, go through a hedge gap opposite. Now take path CR10 bearing half left across a farm track then right between a fence and a screening bund to reach a rail-stile. Turn left over this then bear half right across a paddock and the corner of a field to a signpost on the county boundary and Colliers Lane. Now take path S80 bearing half right across a field to where three hedges meet on a rise. Here climb several steps, cross a farm road and climb more steps to pass through a hedge gap then bear half left following a left-hand hedge through two fields with fine views behind you towards Bennett End and Bledlow Ridge. Where the hedge ends, bear left through a gap onto a parallel farm track and continue along it. By a bungalow to your right leave the track and take path S79 bearing half left across a field and passing left of an electricity pole. Now cross a concealed stile in a field corner and go straight on across an old parkland field keeping just left of several clumps of trees then a fence to cross a stile by a gate. 25 yards further on bear left onto path S92 and retrace your outward route bearing half left by the ˊRoyal Oakˋ to reach the village green and your starting point.

WALK 12   Ibstone

Length of Walk: 5.4 miles / 8.8 Km
Starting Point: Road junction by Ibstone School.
Grid Ref: SU758926
Maps: OS Landranger Sheet 175
OS Explorer Sheet 3 (or old Pathfinder Sheet 1137
(SU69/79))
Chiltern Society FP Map No.11
How to get there / Parking: Ibstone, 7 miles west of High
Wycombe, may be reached by leaving the M40 at
Junction 5 (Stokenchurch) and following the Ibstone
road for 2.4 miles, entering the village and continuing to
its far end. Just past the school at a road junction either
fork right or go straight on and park along the roadside
verge. NB Do not park immediately at the junction on
weekdays as service buses have to turn round here.
Notes: Heavy nettle growth may be encountered in places in
the summer months.

Ibstone, scattered along more than a mile of lofty ridgetop
separating the Wormsley and Turville valleys from Penley
Bottom, until 1895 straddled the Bucks/Oxon boundary with its
church, common and most of its cottages being in Oxfordshire
but, like neighbouring Stokenchurch, the village was then placed
entirely within Buckinghamshire. While the origins of its Saxon
name (spelt ´Hibestanes` or ´Ybestane` in the eleventh century)
are uncertain, it may mean ´yew stone` referring to stones
marking the old county boundary and the native Chiltern yew
trees which seem to thrive on the shallow local soil. There is,
indeed, a particularly fine ancient yew tree in the churchyard of
Ibstone´s tiny twelfth-century church which also boasts a carved
fifteenth-century wooden pulpit believed to be one of the oldest in
the country and a Norman tub font. Being close to London, the
village has, in modern times, attracted a number of well-known
residents including the authoress Dame Rebecca West who lived
at the imposing neo-classical eighteenth-century Ibstone House
near the starting point of your walk.

   The walk, which explores probably the least spoilt area of the
Buckinghamshire Chilterns and offers a series of superb views,

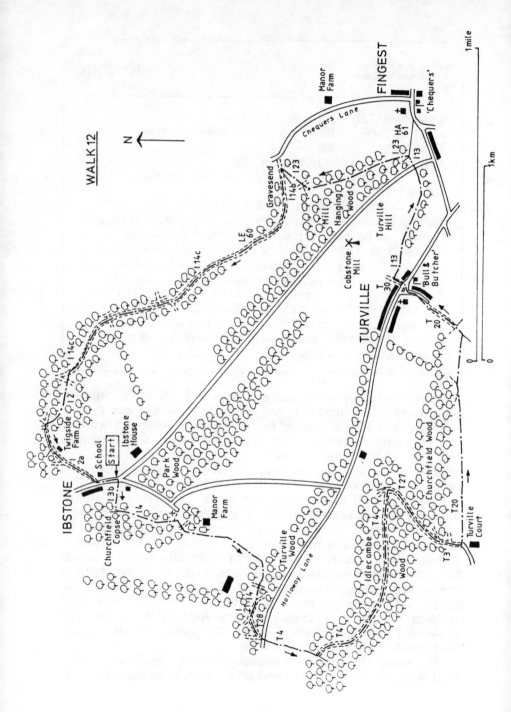

WALK 12

N

IBSTONE

FINGEST

TURVILLE

60

starts near the Victorian village school and passes through woods at the back of the church before crossing the secluded Turville valley to reach Turville Court crowning another high ridge. You then descend to pass through the picturesque village of Turville and skirt Turville Hill capped by Cobstone Mill, an eighteenth-century smock-mill which has featured in many films including 'Chitty Chitty Bang Bang,` and the fascinating village of Fingest before entering Penley Bottom and returning to Ibstone.

Starting from the road junction by Ibstone School, take path I3b off the side-road opposite the school through a hedge gap crossing a stile and following a right-hand fence at first then continuing across a field with views of the squat parish church to your left to cross a stile into Churchfield Copse. Just inside the wood fork left, then at a T-junction of paths turn left onto path I4 parallel to the top edge of the wood, eventually passing Ibstone Church to your left. Just past the church, where the way ahead is blocked, turn right descending steeply through the wood and ignoring a crossing track by a gate to reach a stile into a field by a cattle trough with a fine view ahead across the Turville valley. Here turn left and follow the outside edge of the wood then a left-hand hedge later a fence downhill through two fields to cross a stile into a corner of Turville Wood. The path bears right through this storm-ravaged woodland crossing a concrete road and later joining bridleway I21 which merges from the left and soon enters mature beechwood. Now at a fork go left and take bridleway T28 through the woods to reach a road called Holloway Lane by an electronic gate into the Wormsley Estate.

Cross this road and a stile opposite and ignoring a gate to your right, take path T4 following a right-hand hedge uphill to cross a stile into Idlecombe Wood. Now bear half right onto a timber track then at a fork bear left climbing steeply to a waymarked junction. Here turn left and follow a terraced woodland track along the contours of the hillside for two-thirds of a mile disregarding all branching tracks until you reach a T-junction of tracks. Turn right here onto path T27 and follow this track climbing gently for a quarter mile. On nearing the far side of the wood, at a junction of tracks go straight on (now on bridleway T3) then ignore a branching track to your left and continue to gates at the end of the road by Turville Court, built in 1847 on the site of a house which once belonged to Bysshe Shelley, grandfather of the poet.

Here turn left through a bridlegate onto bridleway T20 bearing slightly left across a field to a gate and bridlegate in the next hedge. Now keep straight on across the next field heading for a tall ash tree on the edge of Churchfield Wood by the far corner of the field. Here follow the edge of the wood straight on with fine views ahead across the Hambleden valley towards the hilltop village of Frieth. Where the edge of the wood bears left, leave it and go straight on past an electricity pole then aim for a group of cottages on the far side of the valley near Fingest until you reach a crossing bridleway. Turn left onto this, soon ignoring a crossing path and entering a narrow green lane. On reaching the end of a road in Turville, go straight on along it to the village green by the church.

Although the name Turville has a French ring, it is, in fact, not of Norman origin, but a Norman corruption of the Anglo-Saxon name ´Thyrifeld` (meaning ´Thyri´s field`) as the village is documented well before the Norman conquest. Indeed the church, whose fabric is in part eleventh-century but has a sixteenth-century tower and has undergone other substantial alterations over the centuries, is believed to have replaced a Saxon predecessor as it has a Saxon font. It is also associated with a gruesome mystery as, during renovation work in 1900, an old stone coffin was found hidden beneath the floor containing not only the skeleton of a thirteenth-century priest but also the remains of a seventeenth-century woman with a bullet hole in her skull! Apart from the church, the village can also boast a fine selection of sixteenth- to eighteenth-century cottages, some of which are half-timbered and some brick-and-flint, and the picturesque timber-framed ´Bull and Butcher`.

Bear half right passing right of the small green then taking path T30 by the postbox up a stony lane. At the far end of the lane where there is a fine view up Turville Hill towards Cobstone Mill, cross the right-hand of two stiles and turn right onto path I13 following a right-hand fence past a garden. By the far end of the garden bear slightly left across the field to cross a stile just right of its far corner where there is a fine view across Turville village behind you. Now take a fenced path straight on through a belt of trees with fine views to your right in places down the Hambleden valley towards Remenham Hill across the Thames in Berkshire. On crossing a stile onto a road, go straight on over a stile opposite to reach a crossways in a corner of Mill Hanging Wood where Fingest´s largely unaltered twelfth-century church with its tall Norman tower with an unusual double saddle-back roof can be seen through the trees ahead.

Here, if wishing to explore the village or visit the ´Chequers Inn`, bear half right onto path HA61. Otherwise bear half left onto path I23 following the inside edge of the wood for a third of a mile with fine views to your right in places across Fingest and the pleasant valley to the north. By the corner of a field to your right the path bears right and passes through a gap in a barbed-wire fence to reach a crossways. Here bear right onto a fenced crossing path and follow it down through a narrow belt of woodland eventually crossing a stile and reaching a crossing track (bridleway I14b) at Gravesend.

Turn sharp left onto this track then, where it forks, ignore a gate ahead and bear slightly right along an obvious bridleway through the tree belt in the valley bottom. At the far end of the tree belt go through a bridlegate and continue along a fenced bridleway, later transferring to the other side of the hedge and continuing (now on bridleway LE60) with fine views to right and left until you reach another wood. Here the bridleway continues along the right-hand edge of the wood at first and then enters it (becoming I14c) and follows an obvious track along its inside edge for a third of a mile ignoring a track merging from your left and branching bridleways to right and left. On reaching a gate and stile, disregard a crossing track and go straight on through the woods. After a further quarter mile turn left onto the waymarked forking bridleway I2 and ignore a crossing track then follow the winding bridleway uphill through a plantation, eventually bearing right to meet a wide track. Turn left onto this and follow it uphill disregarding two branching tracks to your right. On passing through a gate, ignore a branching path to your right and take bridleway I2a straight on, soon joining a road and passing a cottage called Twig Side then continuing steeply uphill with fine views to your left to reach the road by Ibstone School where your starting point is to your left.

WALK 13   Watlington Hill

Length of Walk: (A) 4.5 miles / 7.3 Km
                      (B) 2.4 miles / 3.8 Km
                      (C) 2.7 miles / 4.4 Km
Starting Point: National Trust car park at Watlington Hill.
Grid Ref: SU710936
Maps: OS Landranger Sheet 175
            OS Explorer Sheet 3 (or old Pathfinder Sheet 1137
            (SU69/79))
            Chiltern Society FP Map No.9
How to get there / Parking: Watlington Hill, 1.4 miles
   southeast of the town, may be reached by leaving the
   M40 at Junction 6 (Lewknor) and taking the B4009 to
   Watlington. In the town turn left towards Christmas
   Common looking out for the signposted car park on
   your right at the top of the hill.
Notes: Heavy nettle growth may be encountered on path W4
   (on Walks A and B) in the summer months.

Watlington Hill, protruding for three-quarters of a mile from the
line of the Chiltern escarpment ridge, provides a superb vantage
point for views both along the line of the Chilterns and out into
the Oxfordshire Plain and Thames Valley and as such was an
ideal location for one of the line of beacons warning of the
approach of the Spanish Armada in 1588. Now owned by the
National Trust who have checked scrub encroachment and
created new paths to improve public access, Watlington Hill can
also boast a folly in the form of a 270ft tall obelisk cut into the
chalk hillside by Edward Horne in 1764. This obelisk known as
the White Mark, which can be seen for miles around, is said to
have been intended to give Watlington Church the illusion of a
spire when approaching the town on the Oxford road.

Walks A and B lead you along the crest of the hill with superb
panoramic views before dropping to the Icknield Way on the
edge of Watlington and then gently reascend the escarpment
through scrubland on the north side of the hill to the edge of
Christmas Common, while Walks A and C lead you through
Christmas Common and Watlington Park to descend One Tree
Hill with more fine views across the plain and return by way of

an attractive quiet coombe on the south side of Watlington Hill.

Walks A & B start from the entrance to the National Trust car park at Watlington Hill and bear right through the car park onto a path through a grassy clearing to its far end. Here bear right down steps onto the roadside verge with fine views across the Oxfordshire Plain opening out ahead. Follow the verge downhill for 120 yards ignoring a track to your left then bear left through a kissing-gate onto Watlington Hill. Now take a worn path onto open downland where wide views open out ahead across Watlington and the Oxfordshire Plain and to your right towards Pyrton Hill and Shirburn Hill. Keep right of a belt of scrub on the ridge then continue just below the ridgetop to the far end of the ridge where panoramic views open out in virtually every direction. Here bear slightly right along a grassy path downhill through scrub, soon passing the White Mark to your left. Just past the bottom of the Mark at a path junction bear half right, soon crossing a stile and continuing downhill past a copse to join Hill Road on the edge of Watlington.

Where the ancient Icknield Way, part of the modern Ridgeway Path (W24), crosses the road, turn right onto it for 150 yards. Having rounded a bend, turn right through a fence gap onto path W4 along a sunken way. After 150 yards at a fork bear half left into low woodland then bear right following the waymarks. At another fork bear right to the top of a bank where the path bears left again. At a further fork turn right along a worn path with dense scrub to your right and patchy younger scrub to your left. After 200 yards the path enters thicker scrub and bears left to reach a T-junction. Here turn right and, ignoring a branching path to your left, follow the edge of dense scrub uphill with fine views to your left towards Pyrton Hill and Shirburn Hill. Where the scrub to your right ends, follow a right-hand fence straight on then continue through low woodland dropping into a sunken way at one point and later climbing its left bank, eventually emerging over a rail-stile into a field. Here turn right onto path PY1, part of the Oxfordshire Way, following a right-hand hedge through two fields to a stile onto a road at Christmas Common. Turn right onto this road then at a junction **Walk A** goes straight on while **Walk B** turns right and takes the Watlington road for a quarter mile to your starting point.

Walk C starts at the entrance to the National Trust car park and turns right along the road for a quarter mile to a T-junction at Christmas Common where you turn right onto the Nettlebed road joining **Walk A**. There is much speculation about the source of the name Christmas Common. It is suggested that it might be linked to

65

the prevalence of holly in local woods or even be a humorous reference to the severe weather experienced on the Chiltern ridge in winter, but it more probably refers to the agreement of a Christmas truce here in the Civil War in 1643 when Royalist forces were struggling to defend the ridge against the advancing Roundheads.

Walks A and C now take the Nettlebed road through Christmas Common ignoring a fork to your left and passing the 'Fox and Hounds` to your right. At the far end of the village, just past the disused village church dating from 1891, fork right through wrought-iron gates onto path W8 taking a macadam drive through woods towards Watlington Park. After 100 yards by a clearing to your left fork right onto a mown waymarked path through scrubby woodland ignoring branching paths to left and right and eventually entering Lower Deans Wood, a mature beechwood owned by the National Trust. Here take the waymarked path straight on, disregarding two paths merging from your right. At the far side of the wood the waymarked path bears left and follows a line of ancient beech trees, some of which have succumbed to storms, then crosses a clearing made as a vista for Watlington Park, a large Georgian house to your left with fine views to your right across the Oxfordshire Plain and Thames Valley. On entering further woodland, turn immediately right at a crossways crossing a stile by a gate to leave the wood with more fine views ahead framed by Britwell Hill to your left and Watlington Hill to your right.

Now take a grassy track straight on down One Tree Hill, so-named because of a single ancient yew which stood halfway down the hill, now replaced by a young tree which will take many years to become as prominent. At the bottom of the hill continue over a stile by a gate through a belt of trees ignoring a branching track to your left and reaching a bend in a gravel farm road. Take path W6 straight on along this road for a third of a mile. Just past an old lodge by a brick pillar capped by a white ball and a bungalow to your right, turn sharp right onto path W7 entering an old green lane. Follow this gently uphill for a quarter mile, soon crossing two stiles where you ignore a branching path to your left. Having crossed a further stile, disregard a branching path to your left then at a fork keep left following a line of yew trees to your left uphill through scrub onto open downland. Eventually you enter woodland where you ignore a branching path to your left then follow a left-hand fence uphill to a kissing-gate. Go through this and continue beside a row of ancient beech trees until you reach a branching path to your left leading into the car park.

66

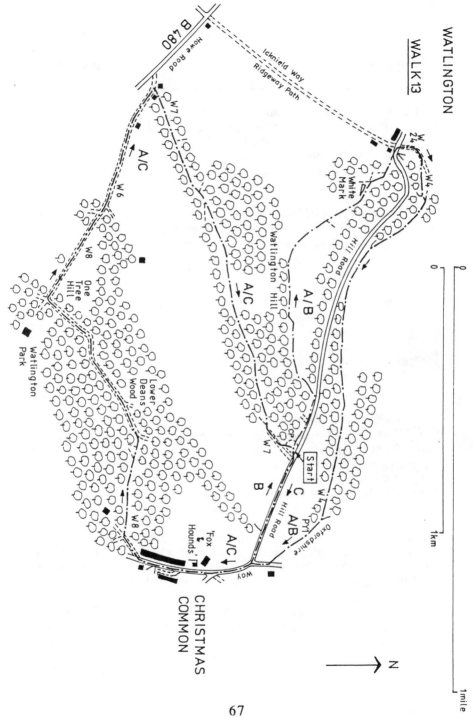

WATLINGTON

WALK 13

67

Length of Walk: 4.6 miles / 7.4 Km
Starting Point: Recreation ground car park, Ewelme.
Grid Ref: SU648912
Maps: OS Landranger Sheet 175
OS Explorer Sheet 3 (or old Pathfinder Sheets 1137 (SU69/79) & 1156 (SU68/78))
Chiltern Society FP Map No.10
How to get there / Parking: Ewelme, 2.7 miles northeast of Wallingford, may be reached from the roundabout at the northern junction of the A4074 and A4130 at Crowmarsh Gifford by taking a minor road signposted to Ewelme for 1.5 miles to a T-junction. Here turn right, then immediately left and left again descending into Ewelme. At a sharp left-hand bend in the village turn right onto a road signposted to Ewelme Down, Swyncombe and Cookley Green and after about 350 yards the car park is on the right.
Notes: Heavy nettle growth may be encountered on paths EW22 and EW24 in the summer months.

Ewelme today is an idyllic sleepy Oxfordshire village with its cottages and old watercress beds nestling in the folds of the foothills of the southern Chiltern escarpment. The village became prominent in the early fifteenth century when the poet Chaucer's son, Thomas, married the heiress to the manor and its fame was increased by their daughter Alice's marriage in 1430 to William de la Pole, Duke of Suffolk. In the years which followed, the Suffolks completely rebuilt the church except for its recently-constructed tower and in 1437 they added thirteen almshouses built around a cloister in the fashion of Oxford colleges and a grammar school which is still in use as the village primary school and is believed to be the oldest primary school building in the country. The church contains a magnificent fifteenth-century carved oak font cover, an alabaster effigy of Alice Chaucer and her parents' tomb with brasses depicting the poet's son and one-time Speaker of the House of Commons and his wife, while Jerome K. Jerome, author of 'Three Men in a Boat' was buried in the churchyard in 1927. On the Suffolks' downfall, the manor passed to the Crown and this resulted in the construction of a palace by Henry VII. This palace was later used by Henry VIII, whose bathing activities led to the pool at the head of the stream (more recently a watercress bed) being named King´s Pool. The palace also served as a childhood home to Elizabeth I but was later sold and allowed to decay so that only fragments of it have survived as part of the present Georgian manor house.

The walk, which is easy in nature and explores the Chiltern foothills around Ewelme, is characterised by its wide open views across the Thames Valley and Oxfordshire Plain towards the Chiltern escarpment, the Downs and more distant hills.

Starting from the car park by Ewelme´s recreation ground, take the lower road into the village passing the fifteenth-century school to your right. At another junction, take the Benson and Watlington road straight on for 70 yards. Just past Greyhound House with the bracket of a former pub sign on its façade, turn left onto path EW22 along its gravel drive. Where the drive bears left, fork right taking a winding fenced path past the garden to a stile into a field. Here follow a left-hand fence uphill with fine views to your right towards the Sinodun Hills ignoring a branching path to your left and continuing, soon with views over your left shoulder across Ewelme and ahead across RAF Benson and Wallingford towards the Downs. At the top of the hill by a large circular lump of concrete, the remains of a wartime gun-emplacement protecting Benson Airfield, turn left onto crossing bridleway EW2 and take this fenced track with fine views towards the Chiltern escarpment to reach Day´s Lane.

Cross this road and take fenced bridleway EW3 straight on between gravel pits in various stages of excavation and restoration to reach the Icknield Way. Having crossed this ancient road, take bridleway EW4 straight on along a concrete track into a green lane, soon with fine views to your left towards Swyncombe Down and Ewelme Down. After half a mile where the track (now bridleway BN18) forks, take fenced bridleway EW5 straight on, then, after 70 yards by an oak tree to your right, fork left into a green lane (still EW5). Some 200 yards further on, ignore a branching green lane to your left and continue gently downhill with fine views towards Swyncombe Down to your left and Ewelme Down ahead to reach a crossways in the valley bottom (where you briefly meet the route of **Walk 15**). Here turn left onto bridleway EW29 and take this stony track towards Swyncombe Down for half a mile. On reaching the crossing drive to Ewelme Down House, take bridleway EW29 straight on following a left-hand hedge gently uphill at first then a right-hand hedge gently downhill to rejoin the Icknield Way in Warren Bottom.

Turn right onto this road then at a sharp right-hand bend near the foot of Swyncombe Down, leave the road and take the Icknield Way (SW34) straight on. After 30 yards turn left onto a crossing farm road (EW14) and follow it straight on for two-thirds of a mile, ignoring a branching farm road and passing Huntinglands Farm with fine views soon opening out ahead towards the Sinodun Hills, Didcot Power Station and the Downs. Where the farm road forks and the main track turns left, take a grassy track straight on. Some 200 yards beyond a lone walnut tree, turn left over a stile by a gate onto path EW24 bearing half right across a field to cross a stile at the near end of a hedge on the skyline left of a council estate. Now take the left-hand fenced path straight on with fine views to your left, eventually dropping past an overflow graveyard to reach a road opposite Ewelme churchyard. Turn left onto this road passing the church and continuing gently downhill to your starting point.

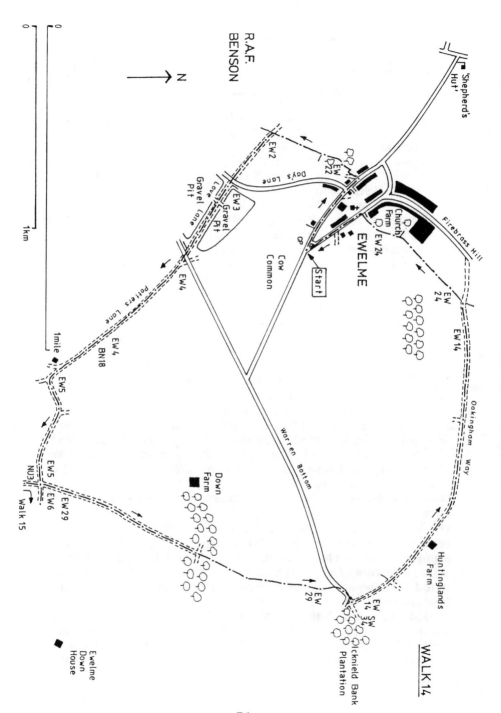

R.A.F.
BENSON

→ N

0 _____ 1km

'Shepherd's Hut'

Firebrass Hill

EW 2

Day's Lane

EW 22

Gravel Pit

Cove Lane

EW 3

Gravel Pit

Church Farm

EW 24

EWELME

Start

Cow Common

EW 4

Potters Lane

EW 4
BN18

1mile

EW 24

EW 14

Oakingham Way

EW 5

Warren Bottom

Down Farm

Huntinglands Farm

EW 5
EW 6

EW 29

NU3

Walk 15

EW 29

EW 14
SW
34

Icknield Bank Plantation

Ewelme Down House

WALK 14

71

WALK 15   Nuffield

Length of Walk: 4.8 miles / 7.7 Km
Starting Point: Nuffield Church.
Grid Ref: SU668874
Maps: OS Landranger Sheet 175
OS Explorer Sheet 3 (or old Pathfinder Sheet 1156 (SU68/78))
Chiltern Society FP Maps Nos. 10 & 15
How to get there / Parking: Nuffield, 6.5 miles northwest of Henley-on-Thames, may be reached from the town by taking the A4130 towards Oxford for 6 miles, then turning left onto a road signposted to Nuffield, Stoke Row and Checkendon. After just over half a mile, turn right onto a road signposted to Nuffield Church to reach the church on the left after some 300 yards. Cars can be parked on wide grass verges east of the church.

Nuffield, with its extensive heathy common most of which is used as a golf course, is today best known for its associations with the car-maker, William Morris, later Lord Nuffield, who from 1933 to 1963 lived at Nuffield Place, which was built in 1914 and parts of which retain the 1930s furnishings he and his wife installed. Morris, who lies buried in the churchyard, indeed took the name of the village not only for his title but also for his charitable foundations such as Nuffield College, Oxford. Although the Domesday Book indicates that Nuffield was only an insignificant detached portion of Chalgrove parish, 6 miles to the north on the Oxfordshire plain, the construction of its church in the twelfth century suggests that the hilltop village had, by then, become a separate parish. This church, indeed, boasts Roman tiles in its walls, a Norman font with a Latin inscription and an early brass dated 1360 depicting Beneit Engliss, after whom English Farm is thought to be named.

This walk, which is generally open in nature and offers you a succession of fine views, explores the countryside to the north and west of Nuffield where the distinct Chiltern escarpment further to the north gives way to a series of long lofty ridges and quiet steep-ended coombes leading down to the Thames.

72

Starting from Nuffield Church, take the quiet country road westwards along the crest of a ridge for two-thirds of a mile with fine views ahead in places towards the Downs, ignoring the Ridgeway Path branching to your left and a path to your right opposite ´Grimsdyke Cottage`. Just before a left-hand bend, opposite the concealed Warren Hill Farm, fork right onto path NU3a along a short green lane to a gate into a field. Now follow a right-hand fence, later a belt of trees, over a rise through two fields with fine views of the Downs in places, later with Wallingford in the foreground. At the far end of the second field turn right through the right-hand of two gates and follow a left-hand fence past May´s Farm to a gate onto the farm drive. Go through this gate and bear right onto the drive following it within an avenue of trees to the A4130 opposite a garage. Turn right onto its nearside verge (which is normally walkable) and follow it for some 270 yards ignoring a turning to your left signposted to Ewelme which formed part of the main Henley-Oxford road until the opening of RAF Benson severed it early in 1939.

Having passed a clearway sign, look out for signposted path NU3 through a hedge gap to your left, then turn left onto this path crossing the A4130 and going straight uphill until you reach a crossing track known as Old London Road which was the ancient route of the Henley-Oxford turnpike road. Turn left onto this track (NU29) with more fine views to your left across Wallingford towards the Downs. After 130 yards near the top of a rise and the corner of a hedge to your right, turn right through a gap in the trackside bank onto bridleway NU3 following a sporadic left-hand hedge over Harcourt Hill with fine views in places towards the Sinodun Hills and distant Oxford to your left, Swyncombe Down ahead and Ewelme Down to your right. On reaching the corner of a fence, take an enclosed green lane straight on past a scrubby plantation concealing what remains of Warren Farm then follow a left-hand hedge straight on to a waymarked crossways in a slight dip where you briefly meet the route of **Walk 14**.

Here turn right onto bridleway EW6 and follow this grassy track along the valley bottom with Ewelme Down to your left and Harcourt Hill to your right. By the corner of a fence ignore a gate to your left and take a grassy track straight on beside a left-hand fence soon enclosed by a right-hand hedge. On emerging into a field, take bridleway SW16 following the right-hand hedge gently uphill. At the top corner of the field, ignore branching tracks to left and right and take a stony fenced track straight on with Ewelme Park House coming into view to your right and a large concealed

73

pond just visible through the left-hand hedge then continue between farm buildings and a white cottage to a signposted crossways. Here turn right onto the Ridgeway Path (SW11) passing the Ewelme Park lodge to your right and continuing along a fenced track for some 300 yards. At a fork by an overgrown pond to your left, bear slightly left, still following the Ridgeway Path, then ignore a branching track to your left and continue along a narrow green lane. On emerging into a large field, disregard a crossing track and bear slightly right downhill (soon on path NU9) heading for a gap in a belt of trees marked by a white post level with the centre of Coneygear Wood beyond. Go straight on through this tree-belt ignoring a crossing bridleway then bear slightly left across the next field heading for a white post just left of the right-hand corner of Coneygear Wood, soon with a view to your left towards Huntercombe Place, now a borstal. On entering the wood, take the obvious path uphill through it to a gate and kissing-gate onto the A4130 at the edge of Nuffield Common.

Bear half left across the road and still on the Ridgeway Path, take path NU9 up a flight of steps then turning right onto a flint drive. Where the drive forks, keep left passing between a cottage and a garage then bearing left to reach the edge of a golf course. Now follow a series of numbered white posts passing left of a tee and through a belt of scrub then bearing slightly right across a fairway to the right-hand end of an area of woodland. Here bear slightly left across a further fairway to a white post where you enter woodland and keep straight on. On emerging onto another fairway, bear slightly left passing just right of a green and through a gap by an oak tree, then bear slightly left across a further fairway towards the right-hand end of the clubhouse. Here bear slightly right to a marker post on the edge of the golf course, then bear slightly left across a field with fine views to your right towards the Sinodun Hills and distant Oxford to reach the left-hand end of a belt of trees where a stile leads you to your starting point.

WALK 15

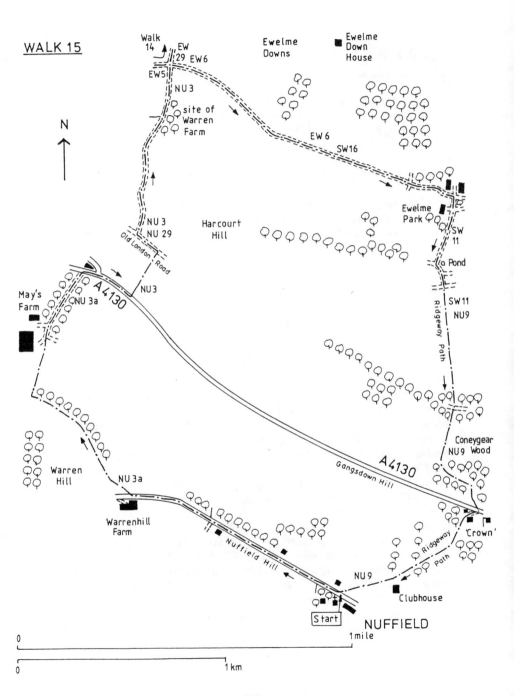

WALK 16 South Stoke

Length of Walk: 4.8 miles / 7.8 Km
Starting Point: South Stoke Church.
Grid Ref: SU599836
Maps: OS Landranger Sheets 174 & 175
OS Pathfinder Sheet 1155 (SU48/58) & OS Explorer
Sheet 3 (or old Pathfinder Sheet 1156 (SU68/78))
Chiltern Society FP Map No.15
How to get there / Parking: South Stoke, 3.7 miles south of
Wallingford, may be reached from the junction of the
A4074 and A4130 at Crowmarsh Roundabout by taking
the A4074 towards Reading for 0.8 miles. Some 300
yards beyond Mongewell Roundabout, fork right at
Icehouse Hill onto the B4009 towards Goring. After 2.7
miles, on reaching South Stoke, take the first turning
right into the village passing under a railway bridge.
Where the road forks, bear left and find a suitable place
to park.

South Stoke, a picturesque Oxfordshire village on the banks of
the Thames with its thatched cottages and a largely unaltered
thirteenth-century church, has sometimes been described as being
on an ´island ` as to the west is the River Thames dividing it from
nearby Moulsford and to the east is Brunel´s high railway
embankment separating the centre of the village from the B4009
and the Chiltern foothills beyond. While the embankment may
appear somewhat overbearing and the peace is occasionally
shattered by the roar of a passing high-speed train, it may, in
fact, be a blessing in disguise as, for most of the time, South
Stoke´s old-world tranquillity has been preserved and what little
modern development has taken place has been largely on the
other side of the railway. Until 1952, like all riverside parishes in
the Oxfordshire Chilterns, South Stoke-cum-Woodcote (as it was
then known) was a long ´strip-parish ` extending for 5 miles from
the riverside up into the hills, but, by then, the hilltop ´hamlet `of
Woodcote had far outgrown the ´mother village ` and so was
given its independence while South Stoke received Checkendon´s
riverside hamlet of Little Stoke in exchange to produce a more
compact parish. As both parishes had preserved the open field

system into the second half of the nineteenth century and neither appears to have been concerned physically to enclose the newly-'inclosed ` fields with hedges, (presumably because their use was already largely arable), the landscape of these Chiltern foothills remains unusually open and therefore offers superb views both towards the Chiltern escarpment to the east and across the Thames Valley towards the Downs to the west.

This walk first explores this open foothill country climbing gently by way of a path recently reopened after being lost for half a century to the top of Watch Folly, some 150 feet above the valley floor where there are superb panoramic views. You then descend to reach the bank of the Thames at Little Stoke before returning along the towpath to South Stoke.

Starting from South Stoke village street in front of the church, take the village street northwards. Where it forks, turn right, soon passing under a railway bridge (which is, in fact, two bridges as Brunel´s original dating from 1840 had to be supplemented by a second when the line was widened from two to four tracks) and continuing to a crossroads with the B4009. Here take the Woodcote road straight on for nearly half a mile, soon with a fine view over your right shoulder towards Lough Down above Streatley. At the top of a rise turn left through a dip in the roadside bank onto path SS10 bearing right across open fields towards the right-hand end of a steep grass bank on the next hillside. Now keep straight on over the brow of the hill passing through a gap in a broken-down wire fence and continuing, now with superb panoramic views, to reach gates on the crest of Watch Folly opposite the middle of a plantation called Cameron´s Copse. This copse was planted on the site of a lone stunted oak tree which for centuries used to cap Watch Folly, from which, varying local legends have it, a boy who had been sent there to keep watch was hanged by the highwaymen or sheep rustlers he was watching for.

Turn left here onto bridleway SS5 and take this grassy track downhill with fine views ahead towards the Downs, Didcot Power Station and the Sinodun Hills to reach Middle Barn, where you ignore a branching track to your right and continue for a further half mile with views to your right towards the large red-brick Fairmile Hospital at Cholsey, the Sinodun Hills and Wallingford, disregarding a branching track to your right and passing a copse to your left. On reaching the B4009, take the Little Stoke road straight on over a rise then down to Littlestoke Manor. By this Georgian manor, which incorporates remnants of a Tudor predecessor such as an oak-framed wall of herringbone brickwork and which passed from the Earls of Macclesfield to Thomas Reade of Uxmore, near Stoke Row, in a land exchange in 1788, follow the road bearing right and continue for a further quarter mile ignoring a branching drive to your left towards Littlestoke Manor Farm. At a road junction turn left onto the road to Little Stoke House. Where it forks by a thatched barn, turn right onto path SS2, a gravel track which once gave access to the former Little Stoke Ferry which carried farm vehicles across the Thames to Cholsey, soon passing Little Stoke House to your left and Ferry Cottage with its unusual evergreen magnolia to your right. Now ignore a branching path to your right and continue to the River Thames at the site of the old ferry.

Now on the Ridgeway Path, turn left here onto the towpath (SS9) and follow it for 1.3 miles, soon entering riverside meadows and later passing under the fascinating skew red-brick railway bridge where, once again, Isambard Kingdom Brunel's original structure from 1840 had to be supplemented with a second parallel bridge when the line was widened to four tracks. You then continue past Moulsford on the opposite bank with its small twelfth-century flint church with a wooden turret which was largely rebuilt in the nineteenth century. On reaching gates into Ferry Lane at the site of the former Beetle and Wedge Ferry named after the riverside inn on the Moulsford bank whose landlord used to operate it, turn left along this raised tree-lined lane and follow it into South Stoke. On reaching the edge of the village, bear right onto a macadam road, then, where this forks, go right for your starting point.

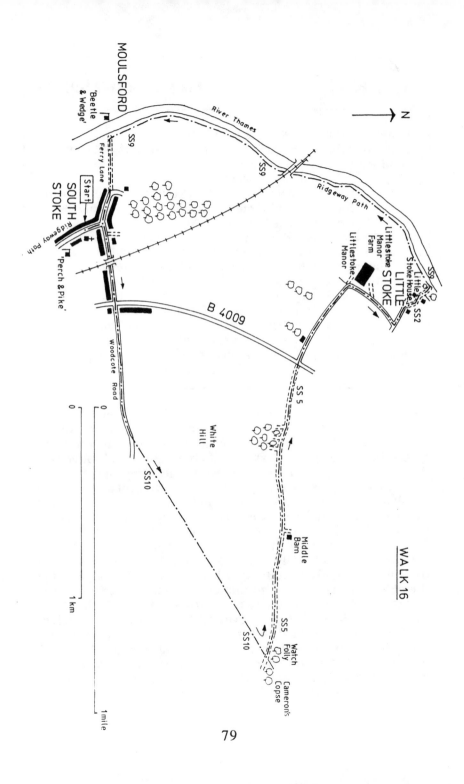

MOULSFORD

'Beetle & Wedge'

River Thames

SS9

SS9

SS9

Ridgeway Path

N

Ferry Lane

Start

SOUTH STOKE

Ridgeway Path

'Perch & Pike'

Littlestoke Manor Farm

Littlestoke Manor

Little Stoke House

LITTLE STOKE

SS2

B 4009

SS 5

Woodcote Road

White Hill

SS10

SS 5

Middle Barn

Watch Folly

Cameron's Copse

SS10

WALK 16

0

0

1 km

1 mile

79

WALK 17   Goring-on-Thames

Length of Walk: 4.8 miles / 7.8 Km
Starting Point: Entrance to Goring & Streatley Station.
Grid Ref: SU603806
Maps: OS Landranger Sheets 174 & 175
OS Pathfinder Sheet 1155 (SU48/58) & OS Explorer
Sheet 3 (or old Pathfinder Sheet 1156 (SU68/78))
Chiltern Society FP Map No.16
How to get there / Parking: Goring-on-Thames, 8 miles
northwest of Reading, may be reached from the town by
taking the A329 towards Wallingford to Streatley. Here
turn right onto the B4009 crossing the Thames into
Goring. There is a small public car park behind the
´Catherine Wheel` in Station Road and another at the
railway station, but on-street parking in the narrow
streets of the town centre is inadvisable.
Notes: Heavy nettle growth may be encountered on paths
GO9 and GO11 in the summer months.

Goring-on-Thames, although, in some ways, resembling other
Thames-side Chiltern towns, has a number of unique features
arising from its geographical location. Situated in the Goring
Gap which separates two ranges of chalk hills, the Chilterns and
the Wessex Downs, where these two ranges drop steeply into the
Thames Valley, Goring has a scenically spectacular setting. This
is enhanced by the wealth of trees on both sides of the river and a
number of islands in the river itself. Goring is also of
considerable historic interest as it is the point at which the ancient
Icknield Way crossed the Thames well before Roman times. It
can boast a substantially unaltered eleventh-century church built
by Robert d´ Oilly containing a bell cast in 1290 believed to be
the oldest in Britain and a number of highly attractive inns and
cottages including the sixteenth-century ´Miller of Mansfield `.
Excavations in 1892-3 also revealed that a nunnery founded in
1181 was once attached to the church but this later became ill-
disciplined and impoverished and following its dissolution in 1536
it was allowed to fall down. In more modern times, Goring
became fashionable in the Edwardian era and this has left a
legacy of neo-Gothic red-brick riverside villas and ornamental

boathouses which characterise the little town to this day.

The walk leads you northeastwards out of Goring through Wroxhills Wood to emerge at a hilltop with superb views up the Thames Valley before descending gently northwestwards to the Thames near the ´Leatherne Bottel `and returning along a raised bridleway, with views of the river through the trees, to reach Cleeve and Goring.

Starting from the entrance to Goring & Streatley Station take Gatehampton Road northwards to a bridge over the railway to your left at the junction with the B4009. Here turn right onto path GO8 along a narrow residential road. Where the road bears right, fork left along an alleyway to a road junction. Here take Lockstile Way straight on. At the far end of the road take macadam path GO8 straight on beside a left-hand hedge then a fence. After 40 yards fork right through a fence gap, cross a road and take fenced path GO9 straight on to cross a stile. Now bear half right crossing a grassy track and another stile then follow a worn path straight on across a field gradually swinging right to reach a stile. Cross this and after 20 yards keep right at a fork passing an old kissing-gate frame and taking an enclosed path for nearly half a mile with back gardens to your left at first and later Battle Plantation to your right, eventually dropping past more gardens to reach Battle Road.

Turn right onto this road then immediately left onto hedged path GO11 left of a gravel drive. Soon the left-hand hedge gives way to a wire fence and views open out to your left across the Goring Gap towards the Downs. On reaching the edge of mature woodland in Wroxhills Wood, the path widens out and bears right climbing to enter mixed woodland. Where the path levels out, ignore a fenced crossing bridleway and take path GO27 straight on, stepping over a low rail and soon passing a clearing to your right. On reaching a crossways of wide tracks, take one of them straight on, then, after 20 yards, fork left onto a winding path through a mature oak plantation eventually reaching Beech Lane.

Turn left onto this unmade county road along the edge of the wood. After 150 yards fine views open out ahead across the Thames Valley and Wallingford towards Didcot Power Station, the Sinodun Hills and the distant Oxford Hills. Here ignore branching tracks to left and right and take Beech Lane bearing left along the inside edge of the wood, eventually reemerging with more superb views of the Downs ahead and Didcot Power Station, the Sinodun Hills, Wallingford and the Oxford Hills to your right. Now ignore a bridleway to your left and leaving the wood behind, take a flinty track bearing right across the fields. Where the track forks by a gas installation, keep right following a stony track in part surfaced with bricks, a few of which are marked with the Star of David, until you reach a macadam road, part of the ancient Icknield Way. Turn right onto this then immediately fork left into a quiet lane and follow its winding course for three-quarters of a mile with fine views ahead towards South Stoke and the Downs.

On reaching the B4009, turn left onto it and follow it for a third of a mile to Spring Farm at the top of a rise, named after the spring which in the early eighteenth century attracted many visitors to Goring due to its alleged medicinal properties. Here turn right into a road signposted to the ´Leatherne Bottel´. Having crossed a bridge over the railway, at a fork keep left, joining the Ridgeway Path, then, where the road turns sharp right and descends steeply to the riverside inn, leave it and take fenced gravel bridleway GO1 straight on for half a mile with views of the Thames to your right in places. Where the bridleway widens into a residential access, keep straight on ignoring branching drives.

On reaching a bend in a road at Cleeve, take Cleeve Road straight on for half a mile into Goring passing Cleeve Mill to your right, parting company with the Ridgeway Path and later passing a recreation ground to your left. Eventually you reach a T-junction with the B4009, Goring High Street, where you turn left. Having crossed a railway bridge, turn right for your starting point.

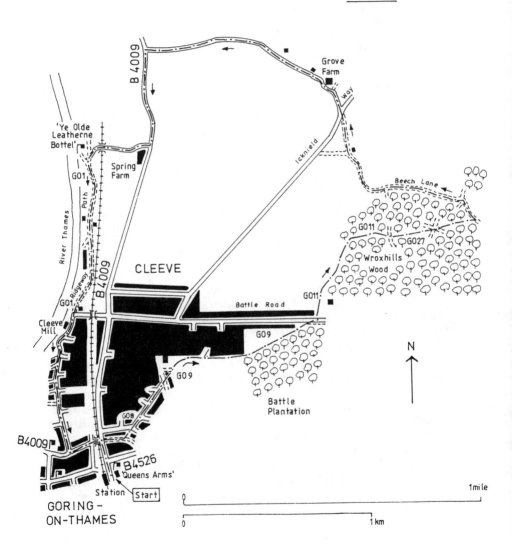

WALK 18   Mapledurham (Chazey Heath)

Length of Walk: (A) 4.4 miles / 7.2 Km
                              (B) 1.7 miles / 2.7 Km
Starting Point: 'Pack Saddle Inn`, Chazey Heath.
Grid Ref: SU695772
Maps: OS Landranger Sheet 175
                OS Pathfinder Sheet 1172 (SU67/77)
                Chiltern Society FP Map No.4
How to get there / Parking: Chazey Heath, 2.5 miles northwest of Reading, may be reached from the town by taking
the A4155 over the Thames, then forking left onto the
A4074 towards Wallingford. After 2 miles, just past a left-
hand turning to Trench Green and Mapledurham, turn
right into a road leading to the 'Pack Saddle` where there
is an informal car park on highway land outside the pub.
Notes: Planning permission has been granted for a large golf
course which, if constructed, may substantially alter the
landscape and make the route description incorrect.
Heavy nettle growth may be encountered on path M7 on
both walks in the summer months.

Chazey Heath, a hilltop hamlet around a coaching inn on the old
road from the riverside town of Caversham to its former county
town of Oxford, is named after the Chazey family who once held
one of the two manors in the riverside parish of Mapledurham.
The mother village of Mapledurham, to which Walk A leads, has
been described as the prettiest village on the Thames and with its
old-world charm and lack of through-traffic it has often been
used as a film-set. Along the village street are a number of
seventeenth-century cottages including a row of almshouses from
1613. At its far end on the right is the fifteenth-century mill with
its wooden tower which is both the oldest mill on the Thames and
the only one which is still working. To the left is the church built
in about 1200 with the tower heightened during extensive renovations in 1862. An interesting feature of this otherwise Protestant
church is a screened-off Catholic chapel belonging to the Eystons,
heirs of the Blount family, the traditionally Catholic owners of the
Mapledurham Estate. Behind the church is Mapledurham House,
part of which is a timber-framed fifteenth-century building, but

much of which was rebuilt in brick by Sir Michael Blount in 1588. This house was visited when new by Elizabeth I and made famous by John Galsworthy who names it as the home of Soames in his 'Forsyte Saga `. Alexander Pope, the eighteenth-century satirist, also visited it and befriended Martha Blount, to whom he left his books, his plate and £1000 in his will.

Both walks explore the pleasant plateau around Chazey Heath while Walk A also leads you through Park Wood with superb views across the Thames Valley to the fascinating riverside village of Mapledurham before returning via Trench Green.

Both walks start from the 'Pack Saddle Inn` at Chazey Heath and take the approach road uphill to the A4074. Here turn right onto its right-hand footway and follow it to the junction with Rokeby Drive. Some 15 yards further on, turn left onto path M10 through a hedge gap with a redundant stile step. Now follow a right-hand fence straight across a field to the edge of Currs Copse where you turn left along it to a stile onto a road. Turn left onto this road then after 90 yards turn right onto path M7, a sunken green lane called Newell's Lane and follow it downhill to a track junction. Here bear right then left and take a green lane uphill to a junction of tracks at the top of a rise where views open out to your left across Reading. Bear left here onto path M6 along a grassy track to a gate and stile where Walk B forks left and takes a fenced track along the left side of a copse called Noke End Shaw. Now read the last paragraph.

Walk A forks right here and takes path M8 along a fenced track on the right-hand side of Noke End Shaw, with the copse later giving way to a rough field. On reaching a stile by an old gateway into Rose Farm, ignore a branching track to your left and bear slightly right joining a concrete road between buildings passing a wooden granary built on staddle stones then leaving the farm and bearing right with wide views to your right across the woods and to your left across the Thames Valley towards Tilehurst. At a junction of farm roads where the concrete road bears left, leave it and take path M5 bearing slightly left across a field to enter Park Wood. Now take a woodland track straight on beside a right-hand fence to reach a clear-felled area. Here leave the track bearing half left and following a right-hand fence at first downhill with a fine view of Purley Park on the other side of the Thames. The obvious path soon bears right along the contours of the hill with fine views up the Thames Valley ahead towards Purley, Mapledurham and Pangbourne beyond and over your left shoulder towards Tilehurst and Reading. Where the path forks, bear half left descending gradually past a folly to your left and through thick scrub, eventually crossing a stile, dropping through more scrub to leave the wood near a redundant stile and continuing downhill to a gate and stile onto a concrete farm road (bridleway M13). Turn right onto this and follow it with views of Mapledurham House and Church to your left to reach the village street at the entrance to Mapledurham.

If wishing to explore this fascinating village, turn left. Otherwise turn right and follow the road round a right-hand bend. At a left-hand bend turn right up some steps and over a stile onto path M4 following a right-hand fence uphill, making sure to turn round for a fine view of Mapledurham village. Now continue past the end of Park Wood and through a hedge gap then follow the edge of the wood bearing right. Where Lilley Farm comes into view on a hill-top between the woods, leave the edge of Park Wood and head for the left-hand end of a long black barn at the farm, going through a gate by the far end of the wood then passing left of a fenced pond and continuing uphill to a gate into the farm. Go through this and keep straight on to join the road by the end of the black barn.

Take this road straight on for nearly half a mile ignoring a bridleway to your right and passing Mapledurham Village Hall to your left. Now with a thick copse to your left at Trench Green, turn right onto path M6 along a concrete drive to Pithouse Farm. Where its surface ends, continue along a rough lane then, where this bears left, go straight on through a hedge gap into a field. Bear slightly right across this field to pass through a hedge gap at the far end of a line of six oak trees then turn left beside a sporadic hedge. Where this hedge bears left, leave it and bear half right onto a grassy track passing right of a line of ash trees then bearing slightly left into a sunken way. Here ignore Newell's Lane to your left and bear slightly right along a sunken grassy track to a gate and stile where you now fork left along the left side of Noke End Shaw.

Walks A & B now take fenced path M6 along the edge of this copse for 200 yards then turn left over a stile onto path M9 bearing slightly left across a field to the centre of a copse in a dip. Here bear half left uphill through the copse past an old gate to a stile. Now bear slightly left across a field aiming midway between a single oak tree and a white cottage with tall chimneys to the left of it to reach an old gateway by a stile into fenced bridleway M15. Turn left onto the bridleway, soon entering Page's Shaw and continuing to a road junction. Here turn right to a T-junction with the A4074 then cross the main road and descend steps right of the junction signposts into the car park outside the 'Pack Saddle Inn'.

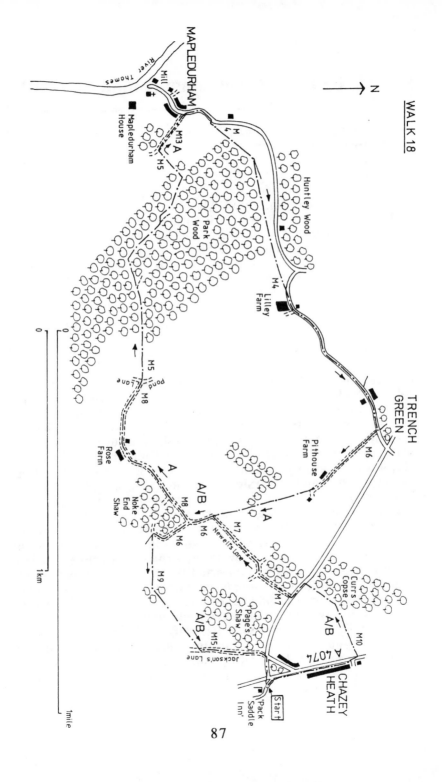

87

WALK 19   Caversham (Emmer Green)

Length of Walk: 5.5 miles / 8.8 Km
Starting Point: Emmer Green Water Tower.
Grid Ref: SU721775
Maps: OS Landranger Sheet 175
OS Pathfinder Sheet 1172 (SU67/77)
Chiltern Society FP Map No.4
How to get there / Parking: Emmer Green Water Tower, 2.5
miles north of the centre of Reading, may be reached
from it by taking the A4155 towards Henley across the
Thames to Caversham, then forking left onto the B481
towards Nettlebed and following it for 1.6 miles through
Emmer Green. On passing the large water tower to your
right, turn right into Tower Close and find a suitable
place to park taking care not to obstruct driveways.

Caversham, as the Reading suburbs north of the Thames are
collectively known, was till the early twentieth century a separate
Oxfordshire town just connected by bridges to Reading on the
opposite bank. In the Civil War an earlier bridge linking the two
was the scene of a battle when the Royalists unsuccessfully defen-
ded Caversham against the advancing Roundheads. Following
Caversham´s absorption into the County Borough of Reading,
however, the small riverside town and the countryside transferred with it, including the hilltop hamlet of Emmer Green, soon
became swamped by the lethal combination of ribbon development followed by infilling which also spilled over into adjoining
areas such as Caversham Park. Since a consolidation of the
boundary in 1977 to incorporate the urban areas, the surrounding Oxfordshire villages, supported by their district and county
councils, have, however, fought resolutely to thwart attempts by
Reading to extend its boundaries further and have thus saved the
countryside beyond the boundary from further incursions.

While Emmer Green may not appear a promising starting
point for your walk, you therefore soon leave it behind and
explore a remarkably rural upland plateau with a scattering of
woodland and fine views at one point across the Thames Valley
to the east of Reading.

Starting from the junction of the B481 (Peppard Road) and Tower Close, go along Tower Close ignoring Phillimore Road to your left. At the far end of the cul-de-sac go through an alleyway extending its left-hand footway to reach Marchwood Avenue where you turn right. Just past house no.12, turn left into another macadamed alleyway and follow it, disregarding a residential close to your left, until its macadamed surface ends. Here turn right into a narrow enclosed path and follow it over two stiles to reach Kiln Road. Turn left onto this then, after 120 yards, turn right into a rough lane called Foxhill Lane. Follow this lane with views to your left towards Dunsden passing Blackhouse Wood to your right then ignoring a branching path to your right and reaching the end of a macadamed road at Littlestead Green. Continue along this road, then, where it forks, turn left into Row Lane then immediately right onto bridleway E30, a stone farm road with fine views across the Thames Valley. After a quarter mile, where the farm road turns left into Dunsden Green Farm, leave it and go straight on past a line of trees to reach a road on the edge of Dunsden Green.

Turn right onto this road then immediately left onto path E20 following a right-hand hedge and ditch. At the far side of the field bear half right through a hedge gap and over a footbridge where an attractive part timber-framed brick cottage comes into view to your left. Here go straight on, crossing a gravel drive and continuing across a lawn to a stile and footbridge into Tagg Lane (bridleway E32). Turn left into this lane and follow it for over a third of a mile ignoring a branching path to your right and reaching the end of a macadam road called Sandpit Lane by Spring Cottages. Take this road straight on then, at a left-hand bend, disregard the first branching path through a hedge gap to your right and 20 yards further on, turn right over a footbridge and stile onto path E27 going straight across a field, passing right of a pond surrounded by willow scrub and reaching the corner of a hedge. Here follow a left-hand hedge straight on for 60 yards then bear slightly right across the field to the corner of a hedge by a wooden electricity pylon and follow this hedge to a gap leading to a road by the 'Coach & Horses'.

Cross this road and take path E13 straight on along a gravel farm road into Comp Wood passing a flooded chalkpit to your right. Where the farm road forks by Comp Farm, bear slightly left keeping left of the farm buildings, ignoring branching tracks to left and right and continuing along a green lane. At a further fork keep left of a hedge and follow this hedge straight on through a large field with fine views to your left and ahead towards Emmer Green with its water tower, Bishopsland Farm and Woodcote on its distant hilltop and through gaps in the right-hand hedge towards Crowsley Park with its radio masts. At the far end of the field continue through a hedge gap and follow the right-hand hedge straight on to a crossing track by an oak tree. Here bear half left across the field corner to join another right-hand hedge and follow it to the far end of the field. Now continue through fence and hedge gaps to join a cottage drive leading to Bishopsland Lane near an unusual single-storey thatched cottage.

Turn right onto this road and after 80 yards , just past a thatched garage, turn right over a stile onto path E33 going straight across a field to a stile into Lady's Shaw. Here take a waymarked path straight on through the wood bearing left and ignoring an overgrown crossing track then bearing right onto path S26 following the edge of Morgan's Wood uphill, later with a fence to your right, to cross a stile into the corner of a field. Now follow the right-hand hedge towards Frieze Farm at Crowsley to a gate and stile. Do NOT cross the stile but turn sharp left onto path S25 crossing the field diagonally to cross a stile by a horse-jump at the right-hand corner of Morgan's Wood. Here go straight on along the edge of the wood then, where it bears left, continue diagonally across the field to cross a pair of stiles between trees in the bottom hedge. Now take path SC9 bearing half right up the next field to cross a stile right of three ivy-clad oak trees and continue through Bird Wood bearing left then right to reach Bishopsland Lane. Turn right onto this to a crossroads with the B481 by the 'Bird-in-Hand`.

Cross the major road and ignoring a signposted path opposite, take the road signposted to Kidmore End and Cane End. At a T-junction turn left into Kennylands Road. After 130 yards opposite a bus stop turn right over a stile by gates onto path SC13 bearing slightly left across a field towards a red-brick building at Chalk-house Green Farm, passing a copse called Cucumber Plantation to your right and (now on path K11) crossing a stile at the corner of a fence. Here ignore rails to your left and follow a left-hand fence to cross a stile by a gate then bear slightly right across a paddock to a further gate and stile. Now bear left following a left-hand fence to cross another stile then continue along a drive to reach Chalkhouse Green Lane at Chalkhouse Green. Turn left onto this road then, where its surface ends, continue along a green lane (K26) following its winding, undulating course for two-thirds of a mile, eventually emerging near riding stables onto a rough road. Take this road straight on (soon on byway RD39) to reach the B481 (Peppard Road) near your starting point.

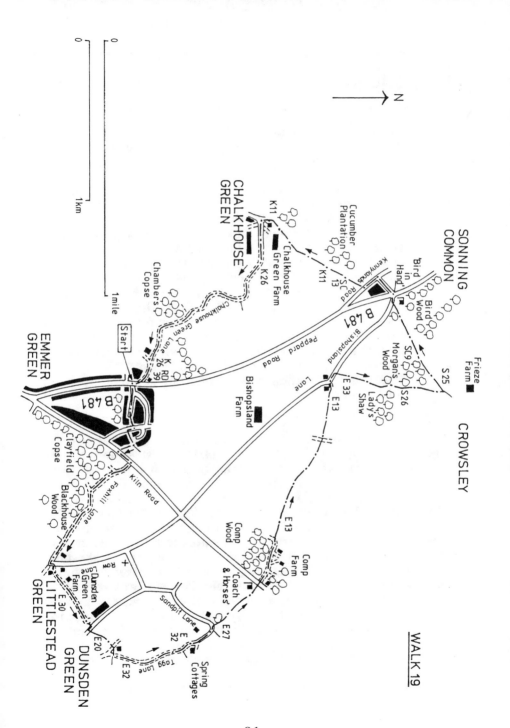

WALK 19

91

WALK 20   Stoke Row

Length of Walk: 5.1 miles / 8.2 Km
Starting Point: Road junction by Stoke Row Church.
Grid Ref: SU678840
Maps: OS Landranger Sheet 175
       OS Explorer Sheet 3 (or old Pathfinder Sheet 1156 (SU68/78))
       Chiltern Society FP Maps Nos. 15 & 16
How to get there / Parking: Stoke Row, 5 miles west of Henley-on-Thames, may be reached from the town by taking the A4130 towards Oxford. At a roundabout just before Nettlebed, turn left onto the B481 towards Reading. A quarter mile past the ´Dog & Duck` turn right into the turning signposted to Witheridge Hill, Stoke Row and Checkendon and follow this winding road to Stoke Row. On entering the village, take its main street straight on past the green and continue to the village school and church on the left. Here turn left into School Lane and find a suitable parking space taking care not to obstruct driveways off this narrow road.

Stoke Row on its upland plateau in the heart of the most heavily-wooded part of the Chilterns is probably best known for its cherry blossom, which briefly transforms an otherwise drab straggling village of mainly Victorian and modern red-brick houses into a picture-postcard scene, and its oriental oddity, the Maharajah´s Well. Built in 1864 with a depth of 368 feet in order to ensure a constant water supply throughout the year, the well was a gift from the Maharajah of Benares to Edward Anderdon Reade of Ipsden House, whose family owned a large local estate, in recognition of his engineering services to Benares and has a canopy in the style of an Indian temple. This well was, indeed, of critical importance to the development of the village as previously Stoke Row, which had only had its own church since the 1840s, had suffered from chronic water shortages and a study of old maps reveals that it was not until the common was inclosed in 1863 and the well was built that the village began to grow to its present size as most of its houses are now located on what, until 1863, was part of the common. It was not until 1952, however, that what had historically been an uphill hamlet of the riverside strip parish of North Stoke and Ipsden inhabited by traditional Chiltern ´chair-bodgers ` (who made chair-legs by hand for the furniture factories in High Wycombe and Stokenchurch) at last became a separate civil parish when a local parish review finally dismantled the strip parishes, a remnant of mediaeval agricultural practice and replaced them with village-based parishes more suited to modern needs.

The walk explores the heavily-wooded country to the south of Stoke Row combining the sylvan solitude unique to the more remote parts of the Chilterns with a visit to the picturesque village of Checkendon with its fine Norman church and ancient cottages.

Starting from the road junction by Stoke Row Church, take School Lane southwards. Just before the last pair of semi-detached houses on the left, turn left past a safety barrier onto fenced path SR22 to enter the curiously-named Hained-in Wood. Here bear slightly right and take obvious path SR23 straight on past a modern house to a brick archway into Busgrove Lane. Cross this road and keep straight on through Common Wood to reach a bend in the Reading road. Turn right onto this road and after 120 yards turn right again onto bridleway C34 and follow this track through Busgrove Wood passing large clumps of rhododendrons then between fields to reach Neal´s Lane at Neal´s Farm.

Cross this road and take path C15 straight on along a stone farm road and former drive to Wyfold Court, until recently used as the Borocourt mental hospital. Just past a bungalow bear half right at a fork onto a fenced grassy track along the edge of Neal´s Wood rounding a slight left-hand bend, then, just after a right-hand bend, turn left onto a waymarked path between rhododendron bushes into the wood. A few yards into the wood turn right onto a crossing track (still on path C15) and follow it parallel to the edge of the wood. On reaching another crossing track, bear half right onto it then, at a junction of tracks by two gates, bear slightly left onto a winding waymarked path downhill through mature beechwood, disregarding a branching path to your right and crossing a stile into a mixed plantation. Here ignore a crossing track and go straight on downhill through the plantation to a fence gap left of a large white house onto a road in Splashall Bottom.

Turn left onto this road then after 25 yards turn right through a gap by a gate (still on path C15) and follow a waymarked woodland track keeping right at the first fork and left at the second. On reaching the edge of a coniferous plantation, bear left and follow an old fenceline for some 60 yards then bear right through the plantation. Ignore a crossing track then bear half left soon leaving the plantation by a footbridge. Now keep straight on, disregarding a crossing track and a branching path to your left then, under a powerline, bear right and follow the powerline to a waymarked crossways near the woodland hamlet of Heath End.

Here turn left onto a crossing track then immediately right. On reaching a gravel road, bear half left onto it and follow it to reach Hookend Lane by a part-weatherboarded cottage. Turn right onto this road then, after some 230 yards by the entrance to Corker's Farm, bear half left into Corker's Lane (bridleway C22). Follow this track through a strip of woodland carpeted with bluebells in Spring for half a mile, ignoring a branching path to your right, passing an old pit, later disregarding a crossing path and finally reaching a road by a cottage. Turn right onto this road then after 120 yards turn left onto fenced path C9 along the edge of a belt of trees with ancient parkland to your left. After 200 yards turn right through two sets of gates onto path C10 and go straight across a parkland field with Checkendon Court, an old manor house restored in modern times built on the site of a mediaeval monastery, coming into view to your left. Now continue past an octagonal brick pavilion to reach gates onto the gravel drive to Checkendon Court near Checkendon Church where the centre of the village is to your right.

Checkendon, despite its remote wooded location, appears to have been the site of a very early settlement as traces have been found of a seventh-century church built in wattle-and-daub at the time when St. Birinus was converting the Saxons to Christianity and built his church at nearby Berins Hill. The fact that the area was always relatively poor has also meant that timber-framed fifteenth- and sixteenth-century cottages, including one with a jutting upper storey, have survived as has the largely-unaltered Norman church considered one of the finest in the Chilterns. Built in the late eleventh or early twelfth century by monks from Bec in Normandy and with a tower and porch added in the fifteenth century, it contains a rare, well-preserved thirteenth-century mural as well as a number of decorative tablets and brasses. Also of interest is a window by Laurence Whistler completed in 1962 in memory of the artist and sculptor Eric Kennington, a friend of T.E. Lawrence, otherwise known as 'Lawrence of Arabia'.

Turn right onto this drive then immediately turn sharp left by a corner of the churchyard wall onto fenced path C11. Ignore a gate ahead and follow the fenced path bearing left, then, where it bears

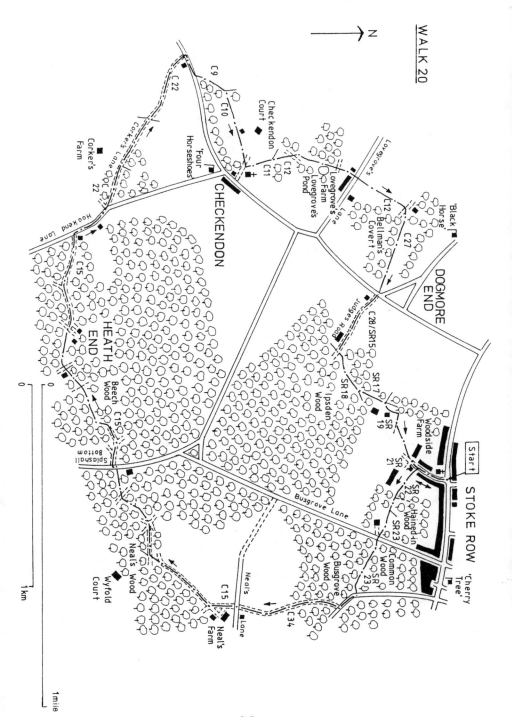

WALK 20

N

95

left again, turn right over a stile onto path C12 bearing left across a paddock to a gate and stile into a belt of trees. Go straight on through the trees ignoring a crossing track, then by two iron gates bear right and take a track beside a left-hand fence at first then straight on through woodland to reach Lovegrove's Pond to your right. Here at a fork take the left-hand option straight on through a gate into a paddock then bear slightly left to cross two rail-stiles flanking a fenced track. Now follow a left-hand hedge straight on, crossing a further rail-stile and taking a concrete path passing left of a garage to reach Lovegrove's Lane. Cross this road and a stile opposite and take fenced path C12 straight on to a stile into a field then keep straight on across the field to cross a rail-stile in the far hedge. Now turn right onto path C27 crossing a stile by a gate and following a track bearing left, ignoring two gates to your right. On entering a field, bear right and follow the outside edge of a wood called Bellman's Covert gently downhill to a gate and stile at a road junction on the northern edge of Checkendon.

Cross the major road bearing slightly left and take bridleway C28/SR15, a macadamed, later gravel lane known as the Judges Road gently downhill to a cottage. The name apparently arises because it was used in the Middle Ages by itinerant judges travelling between the Forest Courts at Ewelme and Wyfold Court which were used to enforce the Forest Law and combat general lawlessness at a time when there was a royal palace at Benson used for hunting in the Chiltern forests, a notorious refuge for outlaws. About 50 yards past the cottage, turn left over a footbridge onto path SR18 following a left-hand fence uphill through Ipsden Wood, a reminder of the former strip parish allegiance of Stoke Row. Where the path forks, keep left and take path SR17, still following the left-hand fence at first, then joining a right-hand fence and following it past a farm. At a slightly-staggered crossways turn right onto path SR19, soon leaving the wood by an old railway wagon and becoming fenced, then turning right between paddocks. After about 50 yards turn left over a stile then bear half right across two paddocks to a rail-stile in the far corner of the second paddock leading to a rough lane (path SR21). Turn left into this lane which becomes School Lane and leads you back to your starting point.

WALK 21   Highmoor Cross

Length of Walk: 3.8 miles / 6.1 Km
Starting Point: Village green at Highmoor Cross.
Grid Ref: SU700844
Maps: OS Landranger Sheet 175
OS Explorer Sheet 3 (or old Pathfinder Sheet 1156 (SU68/78))
Chiltern Society FP Map No.2
How to get there / Parking: Highmoor Cross, 4 miles west of Henley-on-Thames, may be reached from the town by taking the A4130 towards Oxford. At a roundabout just before Nettlebed, turn left onto the B481 towards Reading. A quarter mile past the 'Dog & Duck' turn right into the turning signposted to Witheridge Hill, Stoke Row and Checkendon, where there is a small car park behind the bus shelter on the green immediately to your left.

Highmoor, comprising the hamlets of Highmoor Cross and Highmoor a quarter mile apart on the Reading-Nettlebed road in the most heavily-wooded part of the Chilterns, appears to be a settlement of relatively recent origin as its church only dates from Victorian times and examination of old maps shows that in the 1790s it consisted of merely a few scattered cottages. Indeed, it was only in 1952 that Highmoor was separated from the strip parish of Rotherfield Greys, to which it had historically belonged, which had once extended for five miles from the Thames at Henley to Deadman's Lane northwest of Highmoor.

The walk, which is of an easy nature, leads you from Highmoor Cross through the woods and across fields to the nearby hamlet of Shepherd's Green with its pleasant secluded green before descending into Greys Bottom where a short detour is possible to visit the National Trust property of Greys Court with its seventeenth-century house and mediaeval fortifications. You then return by a largely wooded route briefly crossing open parkland then passing between banks of rhododendrons to emerge near Highmoor's popular roadside inn.

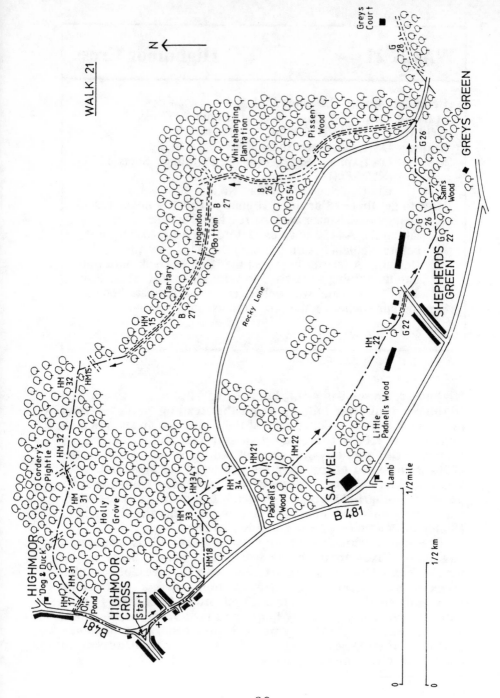

WALK 21

N ←

98

Starting from the village green at Highmoor Cross, take the right-hand footway of the B481 towards Reading past the village church. On reaching The Glebe, cross the main road and continue along its left-hand footway then a verge, soon with a wood called Holly Grove to your left. Just past a cottage (formerly a pub) to your right called ʻThe Woodmanʻ, turn left into Holly Grove and bear slightly right onto path HM18, the right-hand of two woodland paths. Take this ill-defined path through the wood to a T-junction where there are mature coniferous plantations ahead and to your left. Here turn left onto path HM33 between the plantations then, after 100 yards, turn right onto waymarked path HM34 soon leaving the wood by two stiles. Now bear slightly right passing right of a tree and through an area of scrub to cross a stile by a gate into Rocky Lane.

Cross this road and take path HM21 opposite into Padnellʼs Wood, keeping left at a fork. At a waymarked crossways, turn left onto path HM22 passing between hollybushes to cross a ʻstileʻ into a field. Bear slightly right across this field passing left of a fenced pit to cross a stile by a gate by the corner of Little Padnellʼs Wood and follow its edge straight on. At the far end of this copse bear slightly right across a field to cross a stile then follow a right-hand fence to the far end of the field. Here cross a stile by a green gate and take path G22 through the trees onto Shepherdʼs Green.

At this green with its attractive timber-framed and thatched cottages, bear slightly left to join a gravel drive then cross a rough road and bear slightly left to enter fenced path G22 just right of an iron gate. Having crossed a stile, follow the right-hand hedge to cross a further stile into a fenced path into Samʼs Wood. On entering the wood, fork half left onto waymarked path G26, soon ignoring a crossing path and continuing to the far corner of the wood. Here disregard a branching path to your right and a gate to your left and go straight on over a stile into a coniferous plantation. Now take the worn path bearing left, ignoring a branching path to the right and following the inside edge of the wood downhill to cross a stile, then follow the left-hand hedge downhill to a stile into Rocky Lane, onto which you turn right.

Here, if wishing to make a detour to visit Greys Court, take this road straight on for 200 yards, then, at the far end of a right-hand copse, turn left over a stile onto path G28, soon joining a macadam drive leading to the information office. Greys Court, donated to the National Trust in 1969 by Sir Felix Brunner, has had a chequered history. The mediaeval castle, built by the de Grey family from which the name ʻGreysʻ is derived, was fortified by the construction of a surrounding wall in 1348. Four of the five towers and part of the wall still survive. The stables and a donkey-wheel well-house remain from an Elizabethan house built by the Knollys family which was destroyed in the Civil War, but the house which stands here today is of Restoration origin and in design resembles many large Oxfordshire houses.

If not visiting Greys Court, after 40 yards, turn left off Rocky Lane over a stile by a gate onto a National Trust permissive path through Pissen Wood. (NB Should this permissive path be closed, an alternative route using public rights of way is shown on the plan). Follow this wide forest track along the valley bottom for a quarter mile. Eventually it turns left then right and narrows and you ignore a branching path to your left and continue along the valley bottom to a stile. Cross this, turn left through a bridlegate and then turn immediately right onto bridleway B26 following the inside edge of Whitehanging Plantation. At a crossways turn left onto path B27 following a woodland track along Hogendon Bottom, which in Spring is carpeted with bluebells, for half a mile, ignoring a branching path to your left, later becoming path HM15 and eventually crossing a stile into a parkland field. Here go straight on, passing just left of a wooded pit and crossing a raised farm road to reach a low wooden horse-jump just left of the far corner of the field. Cross this and take path HM32 straight ahead into woodland, soon passing a plantation of laurel to your left then a plantation of large rhododendron bushes to your right. On reaching a major crossing track at Cordery's Pightle, take path HM31 straight on. After 30 yards fork right, passing right of a clump of birch trees and rhododendrons and taking an ill-defined path straight on through Holly Grove, eventually reaching the far side of the wood in a slight dip. Here ignore a crossing track and keep straight on parallel to the edge of the wood, eventually reaching a major crossing track (path HM17). Turn right onto this to reach the B481 by a pond which is being restored by the Chiltern Society, where the 'Dog & Duck' is to your right and you turn left for your starting point.

WALK 22   Harpsden

Length of Walk: 3.3 miles / 5.3 Km
Starting Point: Harpsden Church.
Grid Ref: SU763809
Maps: OS Landranger Sheet 175
OS Pathfinder Sheet 1172 (SU67/77) & OS Explorer
Sheet 3 (or old Pathfinder Sheet 1156 (SU68/78))
Chiltern Society FP Map No.4
How to get there / Parking: Harpsden, 1 mile south of the
centre of Henley-on-Thames, may be reached from the
town by taking the A4155 towards Reading. Before
leaving the town, fork right onto a road signposted to
Harpsden and Peppard and follow it for two-thirds of a
mile out of the town and downhill to Harpsden where
you look for a suitable place to park near the church.
Notes: Heavy nettle growth may be encountered in Summer
particularly on path HA8.

Harpsden, which begins less than 200 yards from the edge of the
built-up area of Henley-on-Thames, would seem very fortunate
to have escaped being swallowed up by the Victorian and
Edwardian expansion southwards which took Henley's boundary
to the hillside above the village. Despite this, however, Harpsden,
which actually consists of four separate settlements scattered
along a one-and-a-quarter-mile section of picturesque Harpsden
Bottom, has preserved a remarkably rural atmosphere which
belies its close proximity to the town. Its most interesting and
seemingly oldest settlement is centred around the heavily-restored
twelfth-century church and Harpsden Court, a predominantly
Tudor manor house which incorporates part of a thirteenth-
century hall, but also of note is the black weatherboarded barn at
Harpsden Court Farm opposite the church which incorporates
Regency patterned wallpaper printing blocks apparently brought
to the village when a wallpaper factory closed down.

The walk leads you out of the village uphill through Harpsden
Wood to the Bolney ridge which appears to have been settled
even earlier as the site of an early second-century Roman villa
has been discovered here. You then continue along the ridge to
Mays Green before dropping across a golf course with fine views

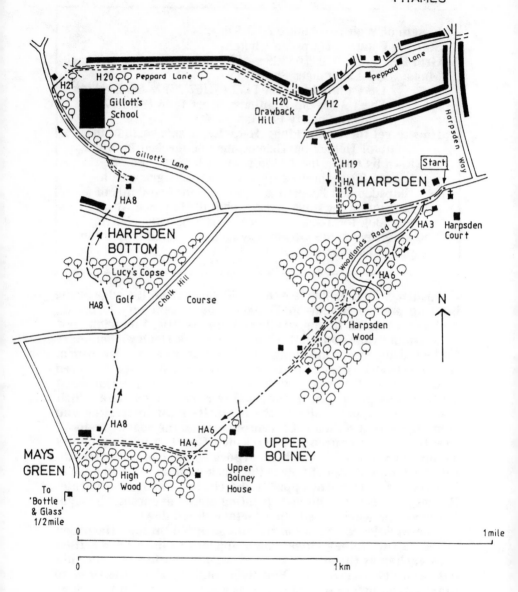

WALK 22

HENLEY-ON-
THAMES

H21
H20 Peppard Lane
Gillott's
School
Gillott's Lane

H20
Drawback
Hill
H2

Harpsden Way

H19
HA 19 HARPSDEN
Start

HA8

HARPSDEN
BOTTOM

Lucy's Copse

Woodlands Road
HA3
Harpsden
Court

HA 6

HA8
Golf
Chalk Hill
Course

Harpsden
Wood

N

HA8
HA6
HA4
UPPER
BOLNEY

MAYS
GREEN

High
Wood
Upper
Bolney
House

To
'Bottle
& Glass'
1/2 mile

0   1 mile

0   1 km

102

to cross Harpsden Bottom, skirt the leafy edge of Henley and descend Drawback Hill to return to your starting point.

Starting from Harpsden Church, take the village street westwards past Harpsden Court Farm noting the wallpaper printing blocks in the barn wall. At a road junction fork left into Woodlands Road, immediately forking left again onto bridleway HA3 into Harpsden Wood. Follow this route, parallel to Woodlands Road at first, climbing steadily and entering a sunken way. Near the top of the hill at a waymarked fork, take path HA6 straight on to reach Woodlands Road. Here keep straight on, crossing the road, following the waymarks and ignoring a branching path to your left and a crossing path. On reaching a gravel drive, bear slightly left onto it disregarding branching drives to right and left. By the entrance to Harpsden Wood Grange, go straight on over a stile by a gate. Having crossed a second stile, keep straight on across a paddock to cross a stile in its far corner. Now continue ahead across another paddock to cross a stile and follow a left-hand hedge through a field to a stile leading to a fenced lane at Upper Bolney.

Turn right into this lane, keeping right at a fork and taking bridleway HA4, a fenced lane along the edge of High Wood, straight on for a quarter mile. Just before a white cottage at Mays Green, turn right through a fence gap onto fenced path HA8. On emerging over a stile into a field, follow a left-hand hedge straight on to a stile onto a road at the top of Chalk Hill. Here cross a stile virtually opposite and take path HA8 bearing slightly left across a golf course, passing right of a pair of mature oaks to reach yellow posts on the edge of Lucy's Copse. Now follow a winding path steeply downhill through this storm-ravaged wood. On reemerging onto the golf course, go straight on downhill to cross a stile and follow a fenced path with views of the Old Rectory to your left to reach the road in Harpsden Bottom.

Cross this road and take enclosed path HA8 straight on uphill. Near the top, look round for a fine view of Harpsden Bottom, then, on reaching a macadam drive, turn left onto it and follow it to Gillott's Lane. Turn left onto this road and follow it for nearly a quarter mile. Having passed Gillott's School and Henley Sports Centre, just before the first right-hand house, turn right onto fenced path H21. At a six-way junction bear half right onto bridleway H20 (Peppard Lane) and follow it for over half a mile with back-garden fences to your left and woodland, later a hedge, to your right. The name Peppard Lane is interesting as it signifies not only that the lane ultimately leads to Rotherfield Peppard, but also as it once formed part of the spine road of the strip parish of Rotherfield Peppard which used to stretch from the banks of the Thames at Marsh Lock for almost six miles through Rotherfield Peppard itself to Wyfold Grange and Kingwood Common, thus suggesting that the lane dates back to at least Saxon times.

On reaching the end of a macadam road of the same name, follow it straight on. Some 40 yards beyond Manor Road to your left, turn sharp right past a safety barrier onto fenced macadam path H2 which leads you to the end of Rotherfield Road. Turn left along this pleasant residential road, then, after about 80 yards opposite the entrance to a house called 'Greysfield', turn right into a green lane called Drawback Hill (bridleway H19, later HA19) and follow it downhill into Harpsden Bottom. Here turn left and follow the road back to Harpsden Church.

WALK 23   Bix Bottom

Length of Walk: (A) 4.8 miles / 7.6 Km
(B) 3.3 miles / 5.3 Km
(C) 3.2 miles / 5.1 Km
Starting Point: Warburg Nature Reserve car park, Bix
Bottom.
Grid Ref: SU720879
Maps: OS Landranger Sheet 175
OS Explorer Sheet 3 (or old Pathfinder Sheet 1156
(SU68/78))
Chiltern Society FP Map No.2
How to get there / Parking: Bix Bottom, 4 miles northwest of
Henley-on-Thames, may be reached from the town by
taking the A4130 towards Oxford for 1.5 miles. At the far
end of a long straight called The Fairmile, turn right onto
the Assendons and Stonor road and follow it for 1 mile to
the far end of Middle Assendon. Here turn left onto a
single-track road signposted to Bix Bottom and follow it
for 1.8 miles, ignoring a branching road to Bix to your
left and continuing to the end of the macadam road where
the Warburg Nature Reserve car park is on your right.
Notes: Heavy nettle growth may be encountered in places on
Walks A and B in the summer months.

Bix Bottom is a long winding characteristic Chiltern dry ˋbottom ˋ
followed by a narrow lane which is an ancient route of the
Henley - Oxford road, but, just as the main road has moved to
the ridge to the south, so the ancient village of Bixbrand has also
virtually disappeared and been replaced by modern Bix just off
the A4130. All that remains of Bixbrand today is Valley Farm
which you pass on Walks A and B and when driving to the car
park and the ruins of its Norman church, abandoned in 1875
after a new church was built in Bix, at the point where all three
walks meet. Aerial photographs taken after the harvest, however,
reveal the outlines of other buildings which explain there being a
church in this deserted bottom. Since 1967 the woodland further
up the valley has been a nature reserve of the Berkshire,
Buckinghamshire and Oxfordshire Naturalist Trust named after
the Oxford botanist, Dr. E.F. Warburg and is notable for its rare

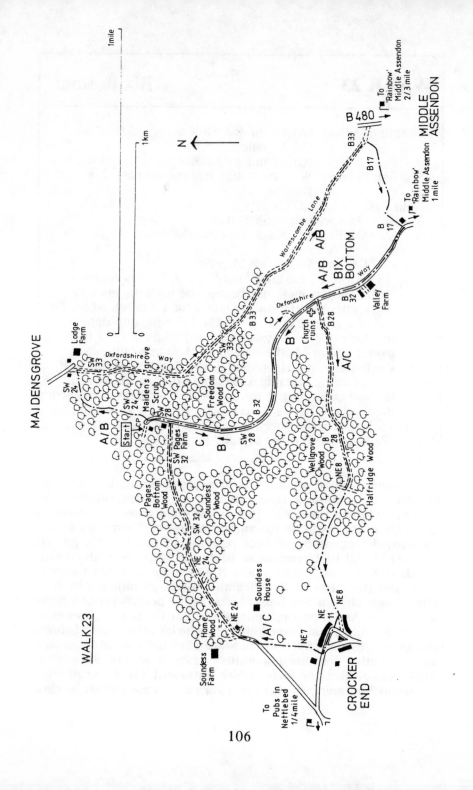

MAIDENSGROVE

WALK 23

Lodge Farm

SW 33
SW 24

Oxfordshire
Maidensgrove
Way
Scrub

A/B

Start

CP

SW SW
24

SW 33

SW 28

Freedom
Wood

B 32

SW Pages
32 Farm

C

B

SW 28

B 33

N

1km

0

0

1mile

1mile

Warmscombe Lane

A/B

A/B
BIX
BOTTOM

Oxfordshire

C

Church
ruins

B

B 32

B 28

A/C

Valley
Farm

Way

B 480

B 33

B 17

B 17

To
'Rainbow'
Middle Assendon
1 mile

MIDDLE
ASSENDON

To
'Rainbow'
Middle Assendon
2/3 mile

Pages
Bottom
Wood

NE
24

SW 32

Soundess
Wood

Wellgrove
Wood

B 28

B

NE 8

Halfridge Wood

Soundess
Farm

Home
Wood

NE 24

A/C

Soundess
House

NE 7

NE
11

NE

NE 8

A/C

CROCKER
END

To Pubs in
Nettlebed
1/4 mile

106

chalkland flora including rare orchids.

All three walks offer you superb views taking you through parts of the nature reserve and passing the ruins of Bixbrand Church, while Walks A and B skirt the hilltop hamlet of Maidensgrove and follow an ancient ridgetop lane called Warmscombe Lane and Walks A and C lead you to Crocker End with its attractive village green and royal connections.

Walks A and B start from the entrance to the Warburg Reserve car park and take the macadam road (SW28) towards Middle Assendon for 30 yards. Now turn left over a stile and take path SW24 through mature beechwoods at first, then joining a left-hand fence and following it uphill through scrubby woodland known as Maidensgrove Scrubs. Near the top of the hill, ignore the stiles of a branching path to your left then go through a squeeze-stile and continue uphill, soon with a field to your left, to reach a stile into Warmscombe Lane (SW33), part of the Oxfordshire Way, near the end of a road at Maidensgrove, described by the well-known Chiltern writer H.J. Massingham in 1940 as 'perhaps the most remote hamlet in all the Chilterns `.

Turn right onto this stony track and follow it for a third of a mile, soon with a fine view to your left across the Assendon valley towards the Buckinghamshire village of Fawley, then following the inside edge of the wood ignoring a branching track into the left-hand field. Where the edge of the wood bears left and the track forks, bear left, leaving the Oxfordshire Way but still on Warmscombe Lane (SW33), and continue along the inside edge of Freedom Wood disregarding a left-hand fork to a field gate. Where the right-hand woodland gives way to fields with a fine view across Bix Bottom, take Warmscombe Lane (now B33) straight on through a ridgetop tree-belt for three-quarters of a mile, eventually descending into the Assendon valley.

On nearing the B480, where a grassy track enters the green lane from your right, turn right onto path B17 following this track uphill beside a left-hand hedge. Near the top of the hill, where the hedge ends, leave the track bearing slightly right across the field with a fine view to your left down the Assendon valley towards Middle Assendon and Henley, crossing the top of the rise to reach a corner of a fence by a stunted tree, now with fine views ahead up Bix Bottom. Here bear half right across the field to a stile then turn left and follow a left-hand hedge downhill, ignoring gates to your left and continuing along a rough track past some farm cottages to gates onto the Bix Bottom road. Turn right onto this road and follow it for over a third of a mile passing Valley Farm and continuing (now on B32) to a branching track near the church ruins. Here **Walk A** turns left onto this track (path B28) joining **Walk C**, while **Walk B** continues along the road (B32, later SW28) following a beautiful bottom for nearly a further mile, eventually passing the much-renovated and extended Pages Farm to your left and reaching your starting point.

Walk C starts from the entrance to the Warburg Reserve car park and takes the macadam road (SW28, later B32) back along the beautiful valley bottom towards Middle Assendon for nearly a mile to reach the ruined church of Bixbrand. Just past the ruins turn right onto a branching track (path B28) joining **Walk A**. **Walks A and C** now take path B28 following a grassy track beside a left-hand hedge past the church ruins then winding its way uphill to a gate into Wellgrove Wood. Here take the track straight on through the wood with a field to your left at first. Where the track forks, take path NE8 straight on. At a second fork, where the main track bears left, leave it and take a wide path straight on, ignoring a crossing track and following the edge of a thick yew wood straight on to a stile into a parkland field where Soundess House, home of Charles II´s mistress, Nell Gwynne, comes into view to your right. Here follow the left-hand hedge straight on for a quarter mile, eventually ignoring a gate to your left and crossing a stile by a gate near a timber-framed cottage on the edge of Crocker End.

Now bear slightly right onto a rough road (bridleway NE11), immediately forking right and following the right-hand edge of the village green to a bend in a road. Take this road straight on, then, just past the postbox where another road merges from the left, turn right onto path NE7 following a gravel drive into a green lane leading to a stile into a parkland field where Soundess House comes into view again ahead. Here bear half left across the field, passing left of a clump of three cedars to reach a gate and stile onto a road. Turn right onto this road and where its macadam surface ends at a three-way fork by Soundess Lodge, take a gravel lane (NE24) straight on past the lodge into Home Wood, ignoring branching tracks to left and right and continuing downhill into the valley bottom. Here, at a crossways of tracks, bear half right onto SW32 taking a stony track down the valley bottom, later with a field to your right to reach the Bix Bottom road (SW28) by Pages Farm, a picturesque, much renovated and extended former farm. Now turn left onto this road and follow it back to the car park.

WALK 24   Hambleden (Mill End)

Length of Walk: 4.9 miles / 7.9 Km
Starting Point: Entrance to public car park at Mill End.
Grid Ref: SU785854
Maps: OS Landranger Sheet 175
         OS Explorer Sheet 3 (or old Pathfinder Sheets 1156
         (SU68/78) & 1157 (SU88/98))
         Chiltern Society FP Map No.11
How to get there / Parking: Mill End, 4 miles west of
    Marlow, may be reached from the town by taking the
    winding A4155 towards Henley-on-Thames for 4.5 miles
    to Mill End, then turning right onto a road signposted to
    Hambleden, Skirmett and Fingest. A public car park is on
    the left just past the turning to Rotten Row.

Mill End, though today only a small riverside appendage of Hambleden, is a settlement of considerable antiquity as the remains of an early Roman villa were discovered here in 1911 and during subsequent excavations of the site, evidence of earlier Iron Age habitation was also found. Today the hamlet consists of the early seventeenth-century Yewden Manor, where the fugitive Charles I sought refuge in 1646, and a number of attractive farms and cottages. What most visitors come to see, however, is the picturesque riverside scene with the lock, weir, watermill and verdant islands, which is often considered to be the most beautiful on the whole of the Thames. Equally popular with visitors is the picturesque mother village of Hambleden which, thanks to the Hambleden Estate and the National Trust, to which much of it is covenanted, has been largely spared from modern development and is therefore regularly used as a set for historical films. In addition to its attractive brick-and-flint cottages and old-world shops, the village can boast a working pump, a Jacobean manor house belonging to the descendants of the Victorian bookseller, W.H. Smith who is buried in the churchyard and a fourteenth-century church with a tower rebuilt in 1721 and heightened in 1883 which dominates the scene when approaching the village.

    The walk leads you from Mill End along the Thames towpath to the fascinating riverside village of Medmenham before climbing over Killdown Bank with its superb panoramic views

109

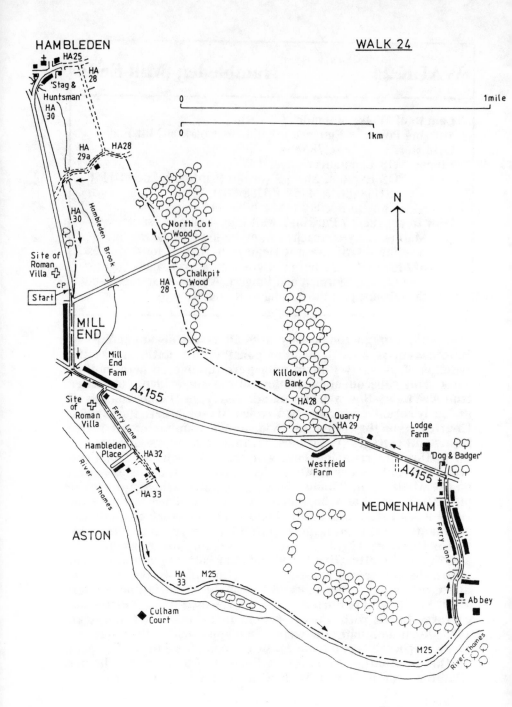

HAMBLEDEN

MILL END

Start

Site of Roman Villa

MEDMENHAM

ASTON

N

0 _____ 1mile

0 _____ 1km

110

first of the Thames and then the Hambleden valley to pass close to Hambleden village, to which you can make a detour if you wish, and return to Mill End.

Starting from the entrance to the Mill End car park, cross the road and turn right along its footway, ignoring branching footpaths and the road to Rotten Row, and continue past Yewden Farm with a plaque bearing the W.H. Smith logo and the date ´1884` to the T-junction with the A4155 at Mill End. Turn left onto its footway and where it ends by Mill End Farm, cross the road and take a narrow path along the top of the roadside bank to a side-turning known as Ferry Lane as it leads to the former Aston Ferry. Turn right into this lane passing a pair of cottages with a crest, the date ´1901` and a clock dated ´1994`, then bearing left. Where the lane forks and the public road turns right towards the old ferry, take path HA32 straight on along a macadam drive ignoring branching drives to your right then crossing a stile into the corner of a field. Here turn right over a second stile onto path HA33 following a right-hand hedge with views to your left towards Culham Court, a red-brick mansion with terraced gardens on the Berkshire bank built in 1770.

On reaching the bank of the Thames, bear left onto its towpath following the riverbank for 1.4 miles with the river largely hidden by trees which have grown up since the use of horse-drawn barges was abandoned. Having passed Culham Court to your right, a close view of which is permitted by a gap in the trees, and gone through a gate into a second field (now on path M25), gaps in the trees give better views of the river and fine views open out to your left towards Killdown Bank and later Lodge Farm, which looks like a castle on its steep-sided hilltop. Eventually you go through a gate and pass a seat and a monument to Viscount Devonport´s Court of Appeal victory in 1899 determining that the now-defunct Medmenham Ferry near this point was public and then cross a footbridge to reach the end of Ferry Lane, Medmenham.

Medmenham, much of which is hidden from the main road along this cul-de-sac lane and so is a haven of rural peace, was the site of a thirteenth-century Cistercian riverside abbey, the remains of which were incorporated in a Tudor house built by Francis Duffield in 1595 and later extensively restored in 1745 and 1898. In the mid-eighteenth century this abbey achieved notoriety when it was rented by Sir Francis Dashwood, who later became Lord le Despencer, and was used for meetings of his Knights of St. Francis or Hellfire Club which were allegedly of an orgiastic nature. Be that as it may, he had the inscription ´Fay ce que voudras` quoted from the French poet, Rabelais, carved above the entrance, which does nothing to dispel the legend.

Leaving the river, go straight on up Ferry Lane with its attractive cottages of various styles and periods, some seventeenth-century, to reach the A4155 by the twelfth-century church with its fifteenth-century tower and chancel. Here turn left onto the A4155 footway and follow it for a third of a mile passing the church and the 'Dog and Badger`, which allegedly dates from 1390. Having rounded a left-hand bend, just before the Westfield turning, turn right crossing the A4155 and a stile and take path HA29 following a right-hand fence uphill through scrubby woodland past an old chalk quarry to your left. Soon after this fence bears away to the right, turn left through a fence gap onto path HA28 following the contours of the hill through the wood to reach a stile onto Killdown Bank. Here follow the left-hand fence straight on with superb views along and across the Thames Valley ahead and to your left. At the far end of the field cross a stile and take a grassy track straight on across the next field, gradually bearing right to a stile in its far right-hand corner. Cross this stile and a farm track and go straight on across another field to cross two stiles left of three scots pines shading a chalkpit. With Hambleden and its valley now coming into view ahead and Mill End to your left, bear slightly right across a further field, passing the bottom end of an outcrop of Chalkpit Wood to cross a stile and descend steps onto the Rotten Row road.

Bear slightly right across this road then (still on path HA28) climb steps, cross a stile and follow a right-hand fence straight on through two fields to a stile into a corner of Chainy House Plantation. Inside the wood turn left onto a crossing path to leave the wood by another stile, then follow a crop break straight on, later with a hedge to your left. At the far side of the field bear half left onto a farm track entering a hedged lane and following this downhill towards a black weatherboarded barn. Where the lane forks and Hambleden is to your right, take path HA29a keeping left and continuing past the barn with fine views towards Hambleden to your right. After 300 yards, having crossed a bridge over Hambleden Brook and passed a stile to your right, turn left over a stile onto path HA30. Now bear right across a large meadow along a slightly-raised causeway heading between a distant cottage and a clump of trees ahead. By a pit, formerly a pond, shaded by the clump of trees, bear slightly right to a gate and kissing-gate in the far right-hand corner of the field to reach a road junction where you turn sharp right for your starting point.

WALK 25   Bolter End

Length of Walk: (A) 5.2 miles / 8.3 Km
(B) 2.5 miles / 4.1 Km
Starting Point: Bend in B482 on Bolter End Common.
Grid Ref: SU800920
Maps: OS Landranger Sheet 175
OS Explorer Sheet 3 (or old Pathfinder Sheets 1137
(SU69/79) & 1156 (SU68/78))
Chiltern Society FP Map No.11
How to get there / Parking: Bolter End, 4 miles southwest of
High Wycombe, may be reached from the town by taking
the A40 towards Oxford for 4 miles. Just past Piddington
turn left onto the road signposted to Wheeler End, Bolter
End, Lane End and Fingest. After 1.5 miles turn left onto
the B482 at Bolter End Common and then after 400
yards at a left-hand bend at the far end of the common,
turn right onto a concrete track and park along its edge.

Bolter End, one of a cluster of 'ends ` west of High Wycombe,
consists largely of a scattering of cottages and farms around a
common and a string of prewar ribbon development along Bolter
End Lane and is best known for the 'Peacock Inn ` at the cross-
roads. Villages named 'End ` may be found all over the Chilterns
but visually they have little in common. However, while their first
name may derive from a local family name, a geographical
feature or even a touch of humour, such as World´s End near
Wendover, they are almost invariably to be found on or near an
ancient parish boundary, where, in the days before local government and planning control, common land was built upon and
new settlements arose and in this, Bolter End would seem typical.

Both walks, which take in some typically picturesque small-
scale Chiltern scenery, lead you through the woods at the back of
the common to Hanover Hill which you descend with fine views
across the hills towards Fingest in places. You then climb through
Mousells Wood before Walk B turns back towards Bolter End
while Walk A continues to Little Frieth where there are more fine
views before circling through more woodland to Parmoor and
the quiet village of Frieth and returning to Bolter End.

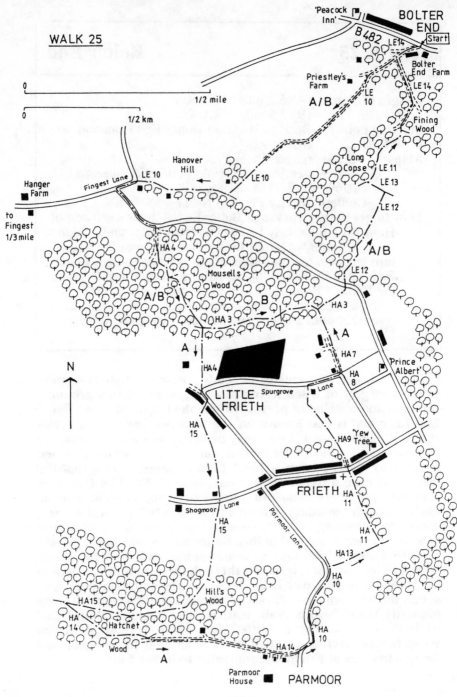

WALK 25

0 _____ 1/2 mile

0 _____ 1/2 km

N

'Peacock Inn'

BOLTER END

B 482

Start

LE 14

Bolter End Farm

Priestley's Farm

A/B

LE 10

LE 14

Fining Wood

Long Copse

LE 11

LE 13

LE 12

Hanover Hill

LE 10

LE 10

Hanger Farm

Fingest Lane

LE 10

to Fingest 1/3 mile

HA 4

Mousells Wood

A/B

HA 3

LE 12

A/B

B

HA 3

A

HA 7

HA 4

A

HA 8

Prince Albert'

Spurgrove

Lane

LITTLE FRIETH

HA 15

HA 9

'Yew Tree'

FRIETH

HA 11

Shogmoor Lane

HA 15

Parmoor Lane

HA 11

HA 13

Hill's Wood

HA 10

HA15

HA 14

Hatchet

HA 10

Wood

A

HA 14

Parmoor House

PARMOOR

114

Starting from the bend in the B482 on Bolter End Common, **both walks** take bridleway LE14 along the branching concrete road. Where its surface ends, take a rough track straight on, ignoring branching tracks to right and left, then continuing on path LE10 between woods. On leaving the woods, bear slightly left to cross a stile by a gate and take a fenced track along the ridge with views opening out ahead towards Cobstone Mill and the Turville valley and to your right towards Ibstone on its distant ridge. Where the left-hand fence ends, take a grassy track straight on through two fields then cross a stile and follow a right-hand hedge then the edge of a copse to the top of Hanover Hill. At the far end of the copse ignore a gate to your right and continue across the field corner to a stile by the edge of a wood. Turn right over this and take a path enclosed by a sporadic hedge gently downhill along the edge of the wood to a stile. Now follow a left-hand fence and tree-belt straight on downhill to a stile leading to a bend in Fingest Lane where there is a seat to your right with a fine view down the valley towards Fingest. Take this road straight on downhill to a junction where you turn left onto the Frieth road. At a corner of Mousells Wood, turn right through a gap by a gate onto path HA4, keeping right at a fork and climbing steeply. At a second fork keep left continuing steeply uphill. At the top of the rise fork left and then right and continue gently uphill through a plantation to a crossing path.

Here **Walk B** turns left onto path HA3 along the contours of the hill for a third of a mile, ignoring a crossing path. At the far end of the wood turn left over a stile to rejoin Walk A. (Now see the last paragraph). **Walk A** takes path HA4 straight on to a stile out of the wood, then continues between fences to a sharp bend in Spurgrove Lane at Little Frieth, where you go straight on. Just past a brick-and-flint cottage turn right through a gate onto enclosed path HA15 past Creighton Cottage to a gate then a stile by a seat with a view towards Skirmett in the Hambleden Valley. Turn left along the fenced path to a stile by a cottage and Shogmoor Lane. Cross this road and a stile by a gate then bear slightly right along a boundary mound downhill to a stile into Hill's Wood. Here ignore a branching path to your left and bear half right along an obvious path for nearly half a mile through the wood, later with a fence to your right. At the far side of the wood cross a padlocked gate with stile steps, where there are views through the trees of the Hambleden Valley, then turn left onto bridleway HA14. Take this sunken way gently uphill, later with views of Frieth to your left. At the top ignore a track merging from your right and a branching path to the left and take a flint track straight on along the edge of the wood.

By a cottage its surface becomes macadamed and you continue for a quarter mile past Parmoor House to reach Parmoor Lane.

Parmoor House, recorded as ´Pyremere` in 1290 and thought to mean ´peartree by the pond`, was until 1948 the home of the Cripps family who became the Lords Parmoor and whose most famous son, Sir Stafford Cripps, was Chancellor of the Exchequer in the postwar Labour Government. Today the house is known as St. Katharine´s Convent and is used as an old people´s home.

Turn left onto this road and at a left-hand bend take path HA10 along its right-hand verge. Having crossed the entrance to a farm road, cross a stile behind the roadside hedge and follow the back of this hedge to the far side of the field. Here ignore two stiles and turn right onto path HA13 beside a left-hand hedge. After some 270 yards turn left over two stiles and take fenced path HA11 to a kissing-gate onto Frieth´s village street by the church built in 1848 as a chapel-of-ease to Hambleden Church and noted for its carved woodwork by the specialist village firm of West and Collier and stained glass by Kempe donated by the Cripps family. Cross this road and take path HA9 straight on along a green lane to a stile into a field. Now follow a left-hand hedge straight on to a stile at the far end of the field, then take a fenced path past two fields to a stile into Spurgrove Lane. Turn right and follow this lane downhill. At a sharp right-hand bend turn left onto path HA7, a lane with concrete wheel tracks. Where the lane bears left, take the signposted path straight on between hedges into Mousells Wood. Just inside the wood turn right over a stile onto path HA3, rejoining Walk B.

Walks A and B take path HA3 straight downhill to a kissing-gate and steps down to a road. Bear slightly right across the road and take path LE12 downhill through a tree-belt to a stile. Here follow a right-hand fence straight on, soon bearing slightly right across a field to the right-hand corner of Long Copse. Follow the edge of the wood gently uphill to cross a stile by a gate. Now take a terraced path straight on beside a right-hand fence. At the far end of the field ignore a stile to your right and turn left onto path LE13 following a right-hand fence to the edge of Long Copse. Here turn right over a stile and take path LE11 along the edge of the wood to a stile at a field corner into the wood, where you should turn round for a view across the valley towards Frieth. Inside the wood disregard a branching path to your right and join a wider track. At a fork, keep left soon ignoring two tracks merging from your right. Now at a fork bear left onto bridleway LE14 through a neck of woodland to emerge onto a track on the edge of Bolter End Common, onto which you turn right for your starting point.

WALK 26   Copy Green (nr. Marlow)

Length of Walk: 4.2 miles / 6.7 Km
Starting Point: Copy Green Cottages at the northern end
          of Copy Green.
Grid Ref: SU830888
Maps: OS Landranger Sheet 175
       OS Explorer Sheet 3 (or old Pathfinder Sheet 1157
       (SU88/98))
       Chiltern Society FP Map No.1
How to get there / Parking: Copy Green, 1.8 miles northwest
   of the centre of Marlow, may be reached from the town
   by taking the B482 towards Lane End and Stokenchurch
   for 2 miles then turning left into Widmere Lane (which
   has nameboards but no signpost). Follow this narrow lane
   for half a mile passing Widmere Farm (where there are
   two unmarked road humps!), then, where the lane widens
   out at Copy Green, find a suitable parking place on the
   roadside verge.

Copy Green, with its few farms and cottages thinly scattered along half a mile of ridgetop cul-de-sac road with a long narrow green and wide views across the Thames Valley and surrounding hills, today seems a lonely place which the world passes by, but it is not without historical significance as Widmere (recorded in 1223 as ´Withemere` meaning ´willow pool``) is an ancient manor of Great Marlow parish and the site of a thirteenth-century priory of the Knights Hospitallers, whose converted chapel forms one wing of the seventeenth-century Widmere Farm.

The walk, which is hilly but well worthwhile thanks to a succession of fine views, takes you to the end of the ridge at Copy Farm before descending into a deep dry bottom known as Munday Dean and climbing again to the hilltop hamlet of Bovingdon Green with its attractive village green. You then continue through woodland at Marlow Common renowned for its spectacular Autumn tints before crossing another deep bottom to the hamlet of Lower Woodend. Your somewhat shorter return route then takes you back across both bottoms to your starting point at Copy Green.

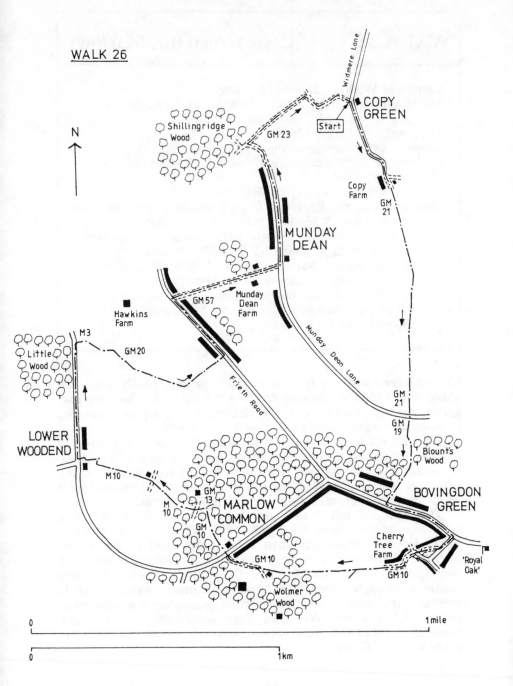

WALK 26

N

Shillingridge Wood

GM 23

Start

COPY GREEN

Copy Farm

GM 21

MUNDAY DEAN

Munday Dean Farm

GM 57

Hawkins Farm

M3

GM20

Little Wood

Munday Dean Lane

Frieth Road

GM 21

GM 19

LOWER WOODEND

M 10

GM 13

M 10

GM 10

MARLOW COMMON

Blount's Wood

BOVINGDON GREEN

Cherry Tree Farm

GM 10

GM 10

Wolmer Wood

'Royal Oak'

0   1 mile

0   1km

118

Starting by the flint cottages known as Copy Green Cottages at the northern end of Copy Green, continue along Widmere Lane to its end at Copy Farm. Here take path GM21 straight on between the farmhouse and stables, continuing across a field to a gate. Now keep straight on over a stile by a second gate, then along the crest of the ridge with panoramic views to your left across Marlow towards Winter Hill and Cliveden, ahead towards Ashley Hill and to your right across Munday Dean towards Marlow Common. Eventually you join the left-hand hedge and follow it downhill to a gate and stile into Munday Dean Lane. Cross this road and a stile behind an old iron seat opposite and take fenced path GM19 straight on uphill, soon skirting Blount's Wood to your left. On reaching another stile, turn round for a fine view up Munday Dean towards Widdenton Park near Lane End with Copy Farm on the hilltop to your right. Now cross the stile and continue past a right-hand wood to reach Frieth Road at Bovingdon Green.

Turn left onto this road and follow it for 300 yards until the village green opens out to your right. Here turn right onto the road across the green then bear half right onto a gravel track to the far right-hand corner of the green. Where the track bears left, go straight on across the grass and the end of a macadam road into a stony lane (path GM10). Ignore a branching path to your left, then, where the lane ends, take a fenced path straight on across the fields looking out for a stile in the right-hand fence. Turn right over this stile, then bear half left to cross another stile. Now keep straight on across the next paddock to a stile in its far corner leading into Wolmer Wood. Take a fenced path straight on through the wood and past a paddock eventually joining a private drive and following it to a road at Marlow Common.

Cross this road and take waymarked path GM10 opposite straight on across the wooded common ignoring all branching or crossing paths. On reaching a waymarked T-junction, turn left onto path GM13, soon crossing a stony track and a stile and taking a fenced path to a stile into a field where there are fine views across the valley towards Lower Woodend. Now take path M10 bearing half right and descending steeply to a stile just left of a barn. Here cross the stile, a farm road and another stile opposite and follow a right-hand hedge uphill to a stile. Cross this and take a winding fenced path to reach a road at the hamlet of Lower Woodend.

Turn right onto this road and follow it for over a quarter mile leaving the hamlet and descending past Little Wood. At the bottom of the hill at a left-hand bend, turn right over a stile onto path M3 following a slight terrace bearing half right up the hill to cross a

119

stile by a gate in the top hedge. Now turn right onto path GM20 following the right-hand hedge around two sides of a field to another stile. Cross this and turn left following the left-hand hedge uphill to a gate and stile onto Frieth Road where rural ribbon development of the type so castigated by the late Chiltern writer H.J. Massingham took place before the Second World War.

Turn left onto this road and follow it for some 300 yards. By a postbox just before a right-hand bend turn right onto bridleway GM57, the drive to Munday Dean Farm and follow it steeply downhill, eventually passing between bollards and continuing to Munday Dean Lane. Turn left onto this road and follow it for a third of a mile through Munday Dean with its macadam surface eventually giving way to stone. On reaching a corner of Shillingridge Wood, turn right into bridleway GM23 following this winding stony lane uphill for a third of a mile to reach your starting point.

WALK 27   Flackwell Heath

Length of Walk: (A) 4.5 miles / 7.2 Km
                     (B) 3.3 miles / 5.3 Km
Starting Point: Mini-roundabout near the 'Green Man`,
                     Flackwell Heath.
Grid Ref: SU894900
Maps: OS Landranger Sheet 175
           OS Explorer Sheet 3 (or old Pathfinder Sheets 1138
           (SU89/99)(Walk A only) & 1157 (SU88/98))
           Chiltern Society FP Map No.13
How to get there / Parking: Flackwell Heath, 2.5 miles southeast of the centre of High Wycombe, may be reached by
leaving the M40 at Junction 4 (Handy Cross) and taking
the A404 towards High Wycombe. Having passed the
Cressex Roundabout, turn right into Daws Hill Lane,
signposted to Flackwell Heath. On reaching the village,
at the mini-roundabout by the 'Green Man` go straight
on, then take the next turning right, Old Kiln Road,
turning right again for the free car park.

Flackwell Heath, (locally pronounced 'Flack'el'Eath`) on its
hilltop plateau separating the Wye Valley and High Wycombe
from the Thames Valley to the south, was till the eighteenth
century largely uninhabited. In the nineteenth and early twentieth
centuries, however, a scattering of cottages and later ribbons of
villas and bungalows gradually lined the Heath's network of
lanes while, in between, there remained green fields and the vast
cherry orchards for which Flackwell Heath became famous. It
was not, however, till after the Second World War that the close
proximity of High Wycombe and London and the scattered
nature of the village's development made it a prime target for infilling and expansion and the green fields and cherry orchards
gave way to the large housing estates which characterise this
suburban satellite of High Wycombe today.

   Despite the unpromising nature of your starting point, both
walks soon leave suburbia behind and descend gently with superb
views across the Thames Valley to the hamlet of Fern near Little
Marlow. You then climb again with more fine views to pass
through Bloom Wood before reemerging near the hamlet of

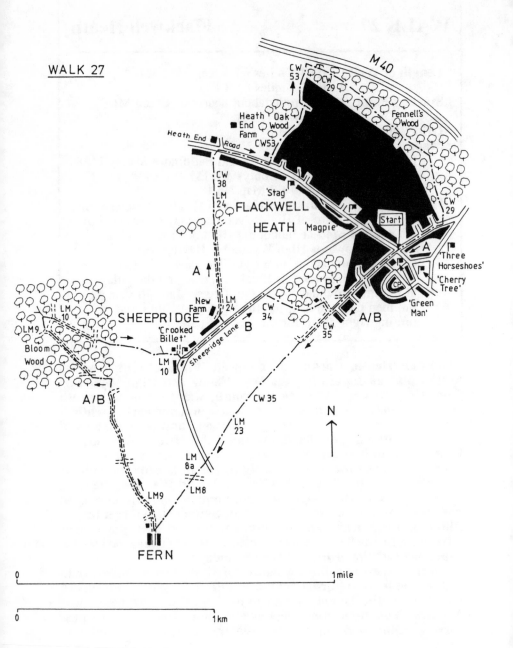

WALK 27

M 40

CW 53
CW 29
Fennell's Wood

Heath Oak
End Wood
Farm
Heath End Road
CW53

CW 38
LM 24
'Stag'
FLACKWELL
HEATH 'Magpie'
Start
A
'Three Horseshoes'
'Cherry Tree'
B
'Green Man'
CW 29

A

New Farm LM 24
SHEEPRIDGE
LM 10
'Crooked Billet'
LM9
Bloom Wood
LM 10
Sheepridge Lane
B
CW 34
A/B
CW 35

A/B

CW 35
LM 23

N

LM 8a
LM 9
LM8

FERN

0 _____ 1mile

0 _____ 1km

Sheepridge with its wayside inn in a quiet Chiltern combe. From here Walk B returns by a direct route to Flackwell Heath, while Walk A climbs to the edge of the village and circles through pleasant mature beechwoods to the north, briefly with fine views across the Wye Valley, to reach your starting point.

Both walks start from the mini-roundabout near the ´Green Man` and take Chapel Road. Where the major road turns left, take Chapel Road straight on. Where this road turns left into Highlea Avenue, take path CW35 straight on along a macadam drive then a fenced track with fine views opening out ahead and to your left across and down the Thames Valley towards Winter Hill and Maidenhead. Eventually you cross a stile by a gate and follow a right-hand fence straight on downhill with Marlow coming into view ahead. At the far side of the field cross a stile and take path LM23 bearing half left across the next field towards some white-painted buildings in the trees at Fern ahead, soon crossing a stile and continuing downhill towards Fern to reach a stile and steps into Sheepridge Lane. Cross this road and a stile opposite and take path LM8a bearing slightly left across a field to the far end of a grassy bank. Here ignore a crossing track and take bridleway LM8 straight on to the far corner of the field where you pass through a fence gap to reach the end of Fern Lane at Fern, an outlying hamlet of Little Marlow.

Here turn sharp right onto path LM9 along a green lane to enter a field. Now ignore a branching track to your left and take a grassy track straight on uphill beside a winding right-hand hedge with wide views to your left across the Thames Valley around Marlow. Where the hedge ends and the track turns right, leave both bearing slightly right uphill to a corner of Bloom Wood. Now turn left along its outside edge with superb panoramic views of the Thames Valley. On reaching a stile into the wood, turn right over it and bear half left through the wood ignoring a crossing track and taking a wide grassy glade straight on for 300 yards until it ends at a crossing track. Turn left onto this then immediately right onto a waymarked path into low scrubby woodland. Where path LM10 merges from your right, turn sharp right onto it to reach a junction of tracks. Here take a grassy track straight on, descending gently for 350 yards, eventually ignoring a crossing track where your track narrows and soon reaching a stile into a corner of a field.

Now follow a left-hand hedge straight on downhill to an oak tree. Here bear half right across a field corner to cross a concealed rail-stile then follow a hedged path ignoring a branching path to your left and a crossing concrete path. On reaching a macadam

123

drive, turn right down it to reach a layby in Sheepridge Lane outside the ´Crooked Billet` at Sheepridge. Here turn left into Sheepridge Lane and where the left-hand buildings end by a wooden cartshed at New Farm, **Walk A** turns left over a stile onto path LM24. Now omit the next paragraph.

Walk B takes Sheepridge Lane straight on, then, at the start of a left-hand bend, turns right up a concealed flight of steps onto path CW34 crossing a stile and following a left-hand hedge then the fence of a cherry orchard uphill with fine views to your right towards Marlow. At the top continue over a stile into a fenced path crossing a further stile, then bearing right onto a macadamed drive, turning left onto path CW35 and retracing your steps along Chapel Road to your starting point.

Just past the cartshed **Walk A** joins a grassy track, soon entering a sunken way and following it gently uphill to a line of trees where the track bears right. Here leave the track and follow a left-hand hedge straight on uphill (later on path CW38). At the top corner of the field continue over a stile and along a fenced path to Heath End Road. Turn right onto this road, then, where the houses begin on its left side, turn left through a kissing-gate onto fenced path CW53 between gardens to reach a corner of Oak Wood. Now ignoring all paths branching left into the wood, follow the back garden fences straight on to reach an outcrop of woodland with large oak trees. Here bear slightly left leaving the fences and continue through the wood to a corner of the wood where you bear right to pass through a fence gap into a fenced macadam path. Turn left onto this path, leaving the wood. Where the macadam path ends, bear slightly left into a field and follow a right-hand fence straight on downhill with fine views ahead across the Wye Valley towards the High Wycombe suburbs of Terriers, Totteridge and Micklefield.

On reaching a corner of Fennell´s Wood, go straight on along its outside edge to the M40 fence then turn right into the wood and follow a path close to the motorway ignoring all branching paths to your right until you reach a path emerging from an M40 subway. Here bear slightly right onto path CW29, gradually diverging from the M40 through open woodland. As the path is ill-defined, until it is waymarked, do not stray too far from the back garden fences on the right-hand side of the wood as the path eventually passes through a scrubby clear-felled area close to the gardens where its course becomes obvious. Having passed through this area, ignore a branching path to your left and bear right to a gap by a gate into Swains Lane where you turn right for your starting point.

WALK 28   Wooburn

Length of Walk: 4.5 miles / 7.2 Km
                     (via Hedsor Church) : 4.7 miles / 7.5 Km
Starting Point: Public car park in Wash Lane, Wooburn.
Grid Ref: SU911878
Maps: OS Landranger Sheet 175
            OS Explorer Sheet 3 (or old Pathfinder Sheet 1157
            (SU88/98))
            (Part only) Chiltern Society FP Map No.13
How to get there / Parking: Wooburn, 4 miles southeast of
    High Wycombe, may be reached from the town by taking
    the A40 towards London to its junction with the M40 and
    A4094 (M40 Junction 3) then taking the A4094 towards
    Bourne End and Maidenhead for 2 miles. Having passed
    the turning to your right for Soho Mill Industrial Estate
    and Wooburn Industrial Park, 150 yards further on, turn
    left by Wooburn Church into a road called Wooburn
    Town. At a T-junction turn left again, then, at a right-
    hand bend, go straight ahead into the public car park.

Wooburn, locally called ´Wooburn Town` to distinguish it from
Wooburn Green half a mile up the valley, was formerly, like its
Wye Valley neighbours, a centre of the paper-making industry
with a tall factory chimney, but in about 1980 the mill was closed
and demolished and replaced by an industrial estate. Despite the
close proximity of this industrial site, the village centre boasts a
number of picturesque timber-framed sixteenth- to eighteenth-
century cottages congregated around its extensively-restored
twelfth-century church with a tower dating from 1442 and it is a
good centre for a number of scenic walks in the surrounding hills.
    This walk soon leaves the village behind and leads you uphill
to explore the scattered community of Hedsor passing its inn and
continuing through woods to a coombe separating the tiny hilltop
church (to which you can make an optional detour) from Hedsor
Tower on another hilltop. You then proceed to pass close to the
Thames near Hedsor Wharf before skirting Bourne End to reach
Cores End and then climbing a hillside with fine views near
Flackwell Heath before dropping again into Wooburn.

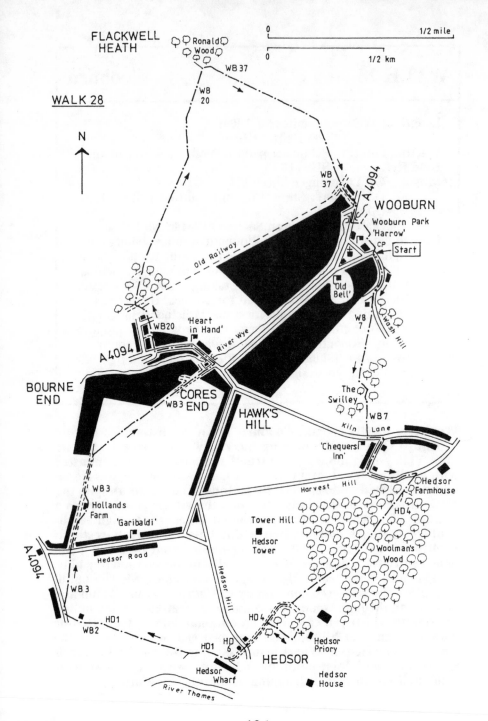

FLACKWELL
HEATH

Ronald
Wood

WALK 28

N

WB 37

WB
20

1/2 mile

1/2 km

WB
37

A 4094

WOOBURN

Wooburn Park
'Harrow'
CP

Start

Old Railway

'Old
Bell'

WB
7

Wash Hill

WB20

'Heart
in Hand'

River Wye

A4094

BOURNE
END

CORES
END

WB 3

HAWK'S
HILL

The
Swilley

WB 7

Kiln Lane

'Chequers'
Inn'

Hedsor
Farmhouse

Harvest Hill

WB 3

Hollands
Farm

'Garibaldi'

Hedsor Road

Tower Hill

Hedsor
Tower

HD 4

Woolman's
Wood

A 4094

Hedsor Hill

WB 3

HD1

WB 2

HD1

HD
6

HD 4

Hedsor
Priory

HEDSOR

Hedsor
Wharf

River Thames

Hedsor
House

126

Starting from the entrance to the car park, turn left into Wash Lane and follow it, ignoring a branching path to the left and rounding a right-hand bend. At a left-hand bend disregard Wash Hill Lea to your right and fork right onto fenced path WB7 along the back of the roadside hedge. On crossing a stile into a field, take the worn path straight on with fine views to your right across Bourne End towards Winter Hill and Marlow and later behind you towards Loudwater. Having entered a wood called The Swilley, take a way-marked path through this wood rich in bluebells in spring, soon bearing right and later left into a field. Here bear slightly right to a stile into Kiln Lane left of the part-timber-framed 'Chequers Inn'.

Turn left onto this road and after 60 yards turn right onto Harvest Hill. Where the major road bears right, turn left into a road signposted 'Unsuitable for Motors'. After 250 yards turn sharp right through a gap by a padlocked gate onto fenced path HD4, part of the Beeches Way, entering Woolman's Wood. Where the path forks, take the Church path and Beeches Way straight on, soon with a deep ravine to your right, into which you later descend. The fenced path then leaves the wood and continues to a kissing-gate onto a private road where there is a fine view of Tower Hill with its eighteenth-century folly known as Hedsor Tower to your right. Take this road straight on past a line of chestnut trees, soon with a view of Hedsor Church, a tiny building with a squat bell-tower almost entirely rebuilt in about 1600, on the hilltop to your left.

If wishing to visit this church with its Russian icon and seat with fine views across the Thames Valley towards Cookham with its prominent church, Cookham Rise, Winter Hill and Marlow, after 130 yards turn left through a kissing-gate and climb the steep field to the right-hand corner of the churchyard hedge, then follow this hedge straight on to a kissing-gate into the churchyard. Otherwise continue along the private road to gates leading to Hedsor Hill. Cross this road and take path HD6 straight on along the macadam drive to Hedsor Wharf passing through the side-gate of ornamental gates. By a second set of ornamental gates bear half right onto path HD1, crossing a stile by a laurel bush and taking a fenced path to a footbridge and stile. Now bear half right across a field to the corner of a hedge then follow this hedge straight on. By a green gate (now on path WB2) bear slightly left and follow a right-hand fence around a Thames Water pumping station to a gate and stile onto the A4094 on the edge of Bourne End.

Cross this stile and turn right, then immediately right again over a second stile onto path WB3, bearing half left beside a right-hand fence to a kissing-gate onto Hedsor Road. Cross this road and take the concrete drive to Hollands Farm straight on. At the farm go through a kissing-gate in the right-hand fence and bear slightly right along a raised track passing right of a cowshed then bearing slightly left to a kissing-gate in a corner of the field. Now continue along a grassy track beside a left-hand hedge to a gate and kissing-gate. Here bear half right across the next field towards the far end of a modern housing estate at Cores End, where you pass through a kissing-gate and follow a left-hand fence along the edge of the estate. Having passed through a further kissing-gate, take a rough (later macadamed) lane straight on, ignoring branching roads to your left, to reach the A4094 near a roundabout.

Turn left onto this road crossing a bridge over the River Wye and passing the ´Heart in Hand`. At the second left-hand bend by a turning called Millside, turn right onto path WB20. Take this alleyway straight on, ignoring a branching alley to the left and crossing the end of a residential road. At a junction of several paths disregard a branching path to your right, cross the former High Wycombe railway (a single-track branch line of the Great Western Railway which opened in 1847 and provided High Wycombe´s first railway link to London but was superceded by a more direct line in 1906 and ultimately closed in about 1970) and bear slightly right up a bank into scrub ignoring a branching path to your left and a crossing path. Eventually you cross an iron stile and bear slightly left across a field to the corner of a hedge with fine views opening out behind you down the Thames Valley towards Maidenhead and upstream towards Winter Hill and Marlow. Now follow the left-hand hedge uphill to the top corner of the field. Here cross a stile by the left-hand of two gates and follow a right-hand hedge through two fields with fine views to your left in the first towards Winter Hill and Marlow, to reach a corner of Ronald Wood.

Here turn right over a stile by a gate onto path WB37 bearing left to a corner of the field. Now bear right and follow a left-hand hedge over the hill with views opening out ahead across the Wye Valley towards Berghers Hill and to your right down the Thames Valley towards Maidenhead. At the far side of the field cross a stile by a gate and bear half right, with views to your left towards Wooburn Green, ahead across Wooburn and to your right down the Thames Valley, crossing a stile by a gate in the far corner of the field and the old railway line. Now go through a gap beside a gate, ignore a branching path to your right and take a gravelly track straight on to the A4094. Turn right along it until you cross a bridge over the River Wye, then turn left onto a path into the recreation ground, skirting the tennis courts to reach the car park.

WALK 29   Farnham Common

Length of Walk: 4.8 miles / 7.7 Km
Starting Point: Northern end of layby on west side of A355
north of Farnham Common.
Grid Ref: SU959863
Maps: OS Landranger Sheet 175
OS Explorer Sheet 3 (or old Pathfinder Sheet 1157
(SU88/98))
(Part only) Chiltern Society FP Map No.13
How to get there / Parking: The layby north of Farnham
Common, 2.5 miles south of Beaconsfield, may be
reached by leaving the M40 at Junction 2 (Beaconsfield)
and taking the A355 towards Slough for 2 miles. Having
passed the turning for Hedgerley and Stoke Poges by the
'Yew Tree`, continue for 0.4 miles rounding a right-hand
bend then turning right into an unsignposted layby.

Farnham Common, straddling the A355 Beaconsfield-Slough
main road is today a suburban settlement with a population of
some 6000, but, as its name suggests, it was once the open
common of the ancient village of Farnham Royal to the south.
Unlike East Burnham Common just across the parish boundary
to the west, which, together with Burnham Beeches, was
purchased by the City of London Corporation in 1879 in order
to preserve it as public open space in the face of the uncontrolled
expansion of the metropolis, Farnham Common fell prey to this
rapacious demand for building land so that all that now remains
of the common is its name.

The walk, which starts just outside the village, explores the
surprisingly rural heavily-wooded plateau between Farnham
Common and Beaconsfield, first passing through Pennlands
Farm in its pleasant hollow, once a centre of the local brick
industry, then following Dorney Bottom westwards across the
A355 to the quiet countryside north of Littleworth Common
before returning through Egypt Woods to your starting point.

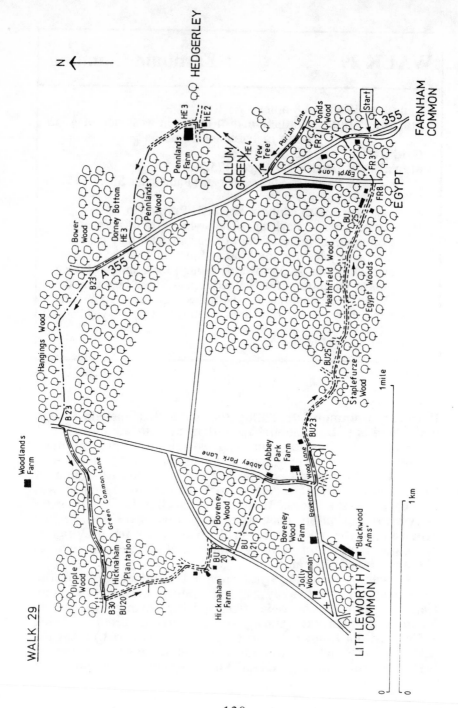

WALK 29

N ←

HEDGERLEY

COLLUM GREEN

FARNHAM COMMON

EGYPT

LITTLEWORTH COMMON

A355

B23

B23

Woodlands Farm

Bower Wood

Dorney Bottom HE3

Pennlands Wood

Pennlands Farm

HE3

HE2

HE3

HE4

'Yew Tree'

Parish Lane

Ponds Wood

FR2

FR3

Start

Egypt Lane

FR8

BU 25

Heathfield Wood

Egypt Woods

BU25

Staplefurze Wood

Hangings Wood

Green Common Lane

Dipple Wood

Hicknaham Plantation

B30

BU20

Hicknaham Farm

BU 20

BU 21

Boveney Wood

Abbey Park Lane

Abbey Park Farm

BU23

Wood Lane

Boveney

Boveney Wood Farm

'Jolly Woodman'

'Blackwood Arms'

1 mile

1 km

0

0

130

Starting from the northern end of the layby on the west side of the A355 just outside Farnham Common, cross the main road and turn left onto its footway. After about 180 yards, having passed some padlocked gates, turn right over a stile onto path FR2 following a right-hand fence through Ponds Wood to a stile into Parish Lane. Turn left onto this road and follow it to the ´Yew Tree` at Collum Green, an eighteenth-century coaching inn. Here do **not** rejoin the A355 but go across the pub forecourt to cross a stile onto path HE4 turning right and following a right-hand hedge and later what is normally a crop-break to a stile where the tower of Hedgerley Church, rebuilt in 1852, can be seen to your right. Now go straight on downhill to a gate at the corner of a hedge at Pennlands Farm.

Do **not** go through this gate but bear slightly left following a right-hand hedge to a gate and stile leading in a few yards to a junction of tracks in the farmyard. Here turn right through a bridgelate by the central gate of three onto bridleway HE2. Just past a barn ignore gates ahead and turn left onto path HE3 following a stony track round the back of the farm to cross a stile by a gate and a cart shed. Now follow a grassy track beside a right-hand hedge across a field to cross a stile by a gate at the corner of Pennlands Wood. Here bear slightly left and follow the edge of the wood through two fields to cross a stile onto the A355 at Dorney Bottom, the name of which reminds us that this was once part of a detached section of the tiny Thames-side parish of Dorney.

Cross this busy road carefully and turn right onto its far verge. At a right-hand bend, where the road enters woodland, turn left over a stile onto path B23 bearing half right and following the edge of Hangings Wood along Dorney Bottom to cross a stile onto another road. (**Beware** blind exit with fast traffic!) Turn left onto this road and almost immediately fork right at a road junction into Green Common Lane. Follow this quiet single-track road for two-thirds of a mile, then, at the far end of Hicknham Plantation to your left, turn left over a stile by a gate onto path B30, a drive to Hicknham Farm. Take this macadam farm road (soon path BU20) straight on along the edge of Hicknham Plantation for a third of a mile ignoring a branching path to your right. At the far end of this wood disregard branching tracks to your left and your right and follow the main drive bearing half right to Hicknham Farm.

At the farm bear slightly left keeping left of the buildings then near the farmhouse turn left along a drive leaving the farm. On crossing a stile by gates, turn right onto a grassy path along the edge of a copse to reach a road. Go straight on along the road for about 50 yards then turn left over a concealed stile onto path BU21 entering Boveney Wood. Here again the name reminds us that the parish of Burnham was once a long strip parish leading from the banks of the Thames at the tiny hamlet of Boveney near Eton up onto the Chiltern plateau and so no doubt this wood once served the inhabitants of Boveney as a source of timber and firewood. Take this obvious, if somewhat overgrown path straight on through the wood for a quarter mile ignoring a crossing path and eventually emerging through a gate into Abbey Park Lane opposite Beechwood House.

Turn right onto this road and follow it past Abbey Park Farm to a T-junction. Here turn left into Boveney Wood Lane, then, at a sharp right-hand bend by Abbey Park Cottage, leave the road and take path BU23 straight on along a stony lane to cross a stile by gates into a field. Follow a left-hand hedge straight on through the field to cross a stile by gates into a corner of Staplefurze Wood. In the wood take a grassy track gradually bearing left and ignoring a branching track to your right, then at a waymarked fork bear slightly right onto path BU25 following a grassy track straight on for over half a mile through Staplefurze and Egypt Woods, going downhill and up again then levelling out and ignoring all branching or crossing tracks. The name Egypt, which appears to be of sixteenth-century origin, is an interesting indication of the history of the area as it does not refer to the North African country but instead is a corruption of the word Egyptians which at that time was used for gypsies, for whom this heavily-wooded area was ideal. On reaching Egypt Wood Cottages, take path FR8 straight on along a concrete road to reach Egypt Lane. Cross this road and a stile opposite and take fenced path FR3 straight on through Prentice Wood to a stile onto the A355 where you turn right for your starting point.

WALK 30   Hedgerley Green

Length of Walk: 4.1 miles / 6.7 Km
Starting Point: Manor Farm, Hedgerley Green.
Grid Ref: SU977879
Maps: OS Landranger Sheet 175 or 176
           OS Explorer Sheet 3 (or old Pathfinder Sheet 1157
           (SU88/98))
How to get there / Parking: Hedgerley Green, 2.5 miles
   southeast of Beaconsfield, may be reached by leaving the
   M40 at Junction 2 (Beaconsfield) and taking the A355
   towards Slough, then immediately turn left onto a road
   signposted to Hedgerley Green and follow it for 1.5 miles
   to a T-junction. Here turn left into Hedgerley Lane
   (signposted to Gerrards Cross) then right into Wapseys
   Lane for Hedgerley Green. Having passed Templars Barn,
   park along the edge of a small green to your right.

Hedgerley Green, a small hilltop hamlet scattered along a quiet
lane which, since the construction of the M40, has been a cul-de-
sac, once seemed a very remote spot only noted for the ghost of
an old lady murdered 200 years ago by body-snatchers who is
said to haunt a sixteenth-century cottage, but today it is difficult to
ignore the roar of the nearby motorway. Its mother village of
Hedgerley in the valley below, which you visit early in the walk,
is not afflicted by this noise, however and despite its close proximity to London has remained a real picture-book country village.
Once a centre of brick-making and the source of the bricks used
by the renowned Victorian railway builder, Isambard Kingdom
Brunel, in the construction of Box Tunnel near Bath, only a local
inn called the ´Brickmould` and the remains of the claypits now
bear witness to this formerly thriving industry. The parish church
only dates from 1852 when a new church had to be built to
replace an earlier building on a different site undermined by
subsidence, but it retains the Norman font from the old church as
well as a fragment of seventeenth-century velvet, reputed to be
the remains of a cloak given to the church by King Charles II as
an altar cloth. Other buildings are, however, older including Old
Quaker House, a timber-framed sixteenth-century building and
Shell House dating from the seventeenth century.

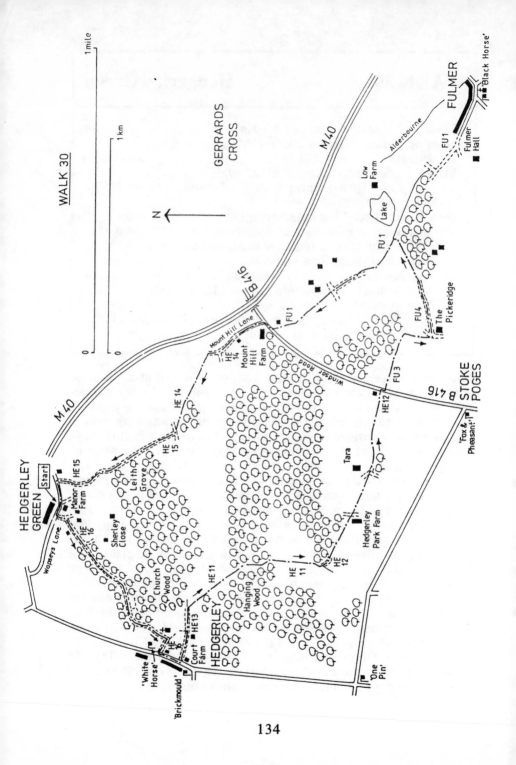

WALK 30

134

The walk first leads you from Hedgerley Green downhill through Church Wood into the picturesque village of Hedgerley before climbing through more woods to a plateau to the south. You then turn eastwards and cross the Windsor Road before descending into the Alderbourne valley above the pleasant village of Fulmer, to which you can make an optional detour. Your return route then takes you up this valley before climbing through more woodland and an old green lane to reach Hedgerley Green.

Starting at Hedgerley Green by Templars Barn and Manor Farm, of which the former was once an outbuilding, take Wapseys Lane (named after a dialect word for wasps) westwards. Just past a large pond shaded by willows, turn left through a gate onto bridleway HE16 keeping right at a fork and following a gravel drive. Where the main drive bears left towards Sherley Close, leave it and go straight on along a wide green lane which soon narrows and enters a belt of woodland. On reaching Church Wood, continue along its inside edge ignoring the stiles of branching paths to left and right and then descending, soon passing Hedgerley Church to your left. By the church gates bear right down a macadam lane to reach gates and a gap leading to the village street near the 'White Horse'.

Turn left onto this road and just past a picturesque pond shaded by a weeping willow, by Court Farm turn left onto path HE13 following a rough lane straight on to its end. Here cross a stile by a gate and bear half right onto path HE11 crossing a field diagonally to a stile into Hanging Wood just right of the far corner of the field. Take an obvious path straight on uphill through the wood then leave the wood by a stile and take a fenced path straight on beside a left-hand hedge. On reaching another strip of woodland, go straight on over a footbridge and through the wood to cross a stile. Now turn left onto path HE12 following a fenced track to a stile then bear slightly right across a field to cross a stile at the near left-hand corner of Hedgerley Park Farm. Here go straight on past the farm buildings then bear half right to cross a stile under a redwood tree. Now bear slightly right across two fields crossing a stile and footbridge and continuing to a stile just left of the top corner of the second field. Cross this and descend some steps then cross a private road and take a gravel drive towards Tara Stud. Now take an enclosed path right of the stud gates through a belt of trees to a stile into a field, then follow a left-hand hedge straight on to a gate and stile onto the B416 (Windsor Road).

Cross this road and turn right onto its footway then turn left over a stile onto path FU3 following a right-hand fence through an area used for sand extraction. After some 300 yards, by an oak tree in a dip to your left, turn right, briefly crossing the workings to enter another fenced path by a stunted oak tree and following it past a further oak tree to reach a concrete road. Here turn left crossing the concrete road and take path FU4 along a fenced grassy track passing The Pickeridge to your right, soon leaving the mineral workings behind and reaching a gate and stile where fine views open out across the Alderbourne valley with its marshy lake frequented by waterfowl towards the M40. Now follow the outside edge of a wood straight on downhill to a gate and stile. Here cross a stile and a footbridge then turn left beside a left-hand ditch to reach another stile.

Here, if wishing to visit the picturesque village of Fulmer with its eighteenth-century inn, its red-brick church built in 1610 by Sir Marmaduke Dayrell and an array of attractive cottages, turn right onto path FU1 and follow this obvious path for half a mile to reach the centre of the village. Otherwise turn left over the stile, also joining path FU1, and follow this path between fences and hedges eventually crossing a stile and emerging near an old flooded gravel pit. Here join a gravel track and follow it straight on to a junction of tracks near some riding stables where military vehicles are stored. Now ignore a crossing track and go straight on crossing a wooden fence and following a fenced path soon between an old orchard and horse paddocks, eventually reaching the B416.

Turn right onto its footway then, before reaching the M40 bridge, turn left into Mount Hill Lane. Where the road ends, take path HE14 straight on over a stile by a gate to follow the former continuation of the road. Near its end ignore gates to your left then turn left over a stile by a gate and follow a left-hand hedge then the edge of a copse to a stile. Cross this and bear half right over a second stile into fenced bridleway HE15 following a right-hand hedge uphill into a wood called Leith Grove. Now continue uphill along the inside edge of the wood, eventually leaving the wood and continuing between hedges where you ignore gates into adjacent fields then, on reaching Wapseys Lane, turn left for your starting point.

INDEX OF PLACE NAMES

Books Published by
THE BOOK CASTLE

JOURNEYS INTO BEDFORDSHIRE: Anthony Mackay.
Foreword by The Marquess of Tavistock, Woburn Abbey.
A lavish book of over 150 evocative ink drawings.

A PILGRIMAGE IN HERTFORDSHIRE: H. M. Alderman.
Classic, between-the-wars tour round the county, embellished
with line drawings.

**COUNTRYSIDE CYCLING IN BEDFORDSHIRE,
BUCKINGHAMSHIRE and HERTFORDSHIRE:** Mick Payne.
Twenty rides on- and off-road for all the family.

LOCAL WALKS: South Bedfordshire and North Chilterns:
Vaughan Basham. Twenty-seven thematic circular walks.

LOCAL WALKS: North and Mid-Bedfordshire:
Vaughan Basham. Twenty-five thematic circular walks.

FAMILY WALKS: Chilterns South: Nick Moon.
Thirty 3 to 5 mile circular walks.

**CHILTERN WALKS: Hertfordshire, Bedfordshire and
North Buckinghamshire:** Nick Moon.
CHILTERN WALKS: Buckinghamshire: Nick Moon.
**CHILTERN WALKS: Oxfordshire and
West Buckinghamshire:** Nick Moon.
A trilogy of circular walks, in association with the Chiltern
Society. Each volume contains thirty circular walks.

**OXFORDSHIRE WALKS:
Oxford, the Cotswolds and the Cherwell Valley:** Nick Moon.
**OXFORDSHIRE WALKS:
Oxford, the Downs and the Thames Valley:** Nick Moon.
Two volumes that complement Chiltern Walks: Oxfordshire
and complete coverage of the county, in association with the
Oxford Fieldpaths Society. Thirty circular walks in each.

**FOLK: Characters and Events in the History
of Bedfordshire and Northamptonshire:** Vivienne Evans.
Anthology about people of yesteryear – arranged alphabetically
by village or town.

**LEGACIES:
Tales and Legends of Bedfordshire and Hertfordshire:**
Vic Lea. Twenty-five mysteries and stories based on fact,
including Luton Town Football Club. Many photographs.

MANORS and MAYHEM, PAUPERS and POLITICS:
Tales from Four Shires: Beds., Bucks., Herts.,
and Northants.: John Houghton.
Little-known historical snippets and stories.

MYTHS and WITCHES, PEOPLE and POLITICS:
Tales from Four Shires: Bucks., Beds., Herts.,
and Northants.: John Houghton.
Anthology of strange but true historical events.

ECCENTRICS and VILLAINS, HAUNTINGS and HEROES:
Tales from Four Shires: Northants., Beds.,
Bucks., and Herts.: John Houghton.
True incidents and curious events covering one thousand years.

THE RAILWAY AGE IN BEDFORDSHIRE: Fred Cockman.
Classic, illustrated acount of early railway history.

CHILTERN ARCHAEOLOGY: RECENT WORK:
A Handbook for the Next Decade: edited by Robin Holgate.
The latest views, results and excavations by twenty-three
leading archaeologists throughout the Chilterns.

WHIPSNADE WILD ANIMAL PARK: 'MY AFRICA': Lucy Pendar.
Foreword by Andrew Forbes. Introduction by Gerald Durrell.
Inside story of sixty years of the Park's animals and people –
full of anecdotes, photographs and drawings.

DUNSTABLE WITH THE PRIORY, 1100–1550: Vivienne Evans.
Dramatic growth of Henry I's important new town around a
major crossroads.

DUNSTABLE DECADE: THE EIGHTIES:
A Collection of Photographs: Pat Lovering.
A souvenir book of nearly 300 pictures of people and events in
the 1980s.

DUNSTABLE IN DETAIL: Nigel Benson.
A hundred of the town's buildings and features, plus town trail
map.

OLD DUNSTABLE: Bill Twaddle.
A new edition of this collection of early photographs.

BOURNE and BRED:
A Dunstable Boyhood Between the Wars: Colin Bourne.
An elegantly written, well-illustrated book capturing the spirit
of the town over fifty years ago.

ROYAL HOUGHTON: Pat Lovering.
Illustrated history of Houghton Regis from the earliest times to
the present.

BEDFORDSHIRE'S YESTERYEARS Vol. 1:
The Family, Childhood and Schooldays:
Brenda Fraser-Newstead.
Unusual early 20th century reminiscences, with private photographs.

BEDFORDSHIRE'S YESTERYEARS Vol. 2:
The Rural Scene: Brenda Fraser-Newstead.
Vivid first-hand accounts of country life two or three generations ago.

BEDFORDSHIRE'S YESTERYEARS Vol. 3:
Craftsmen and Trades People:
Brenda Fraser-Newstead.
Fascinating recollections over several generations practising many vanishing crafts and trades.

BEDFORDSHIRE'S YESTERYEARS Vol. 4:
War Times and Civil Matters:
Brenda Fraser-Newstead.
Two World Wars, plus transport, law and order, etc.

THE CHANGING FACE OF LUTON:
An Illustrated History:
Stephen Bunker, Robin Holgate and Marian Nichols.
Luton's development from earliest times to the present busy industrial town. Illustrated in colour and monochrome. The three authors from Luton Museum are all experts in local history, archaeology, crafts and social history.

THE MEN WHO WORE STRAW HELMETS:
Policing Luton, 1840–1974: Tom Madigan.
Meticulously chronicled history; dozens of rare photographs; author served in Luton Police for nearly fifty years.

BETWEEN THE HILLS:
The Story of Lilley, a Chiltern Village: Roy Pinnock.
A priceless piece of our heritage – the rural beauty remains but the customs and way of life described here have largely disappeared.

GLEANINGS REVISITED:
Nostalgic Thoughts of a Bedfordshire's Farmer's Boy:
E W O'Dell.
His own sketches and early photographs adorn this lively account of rural Bedfordshire in days gone by.

FARM OF MY CHILDHOOD, 1925–1947: Mary Roberts.
An almost vanished lifestyle on a remote farm near Flitwick.

THE VALE OF THE NIGHTINGALE:
The True Story of a Harpenden Family: Molly Andrews.
Victorian times to the present day in this lovely village.

THE TALL HITCHIN SERGEANT:
A Victorian Crime Novel based on fact: Edgar Newman.
Mixes real police officers and authentic background with an exciting storyline.

THE TALL HITCHIN INSPECTOR'S CASEBOOK:
A Victorian Crime Novel based on fact: Edgar Newman.
Worthies of the time encounter more archetypal villains.

LEAFING THROUGH LITERATURE: Writer's Lives
in Hertfordshire and Bedfordshire: David Carroll.
Illustrated short biographies of many famous authors and their connections with these counties.

THE HILL OF THE MARTYR: An Architectural History
of St. Albans Abbey: Eileen Roberts.
Scholarly and readable chronological narrative history of Hertfordshire and Bedfordshire's famous cathedral. Fully illustrated with photographs and plans.

SPECIALLY FOR CHILDREN

VILLA BELOW THE KNOLLS:
A Story of Roman Britain: Michael Dundrow.
An exciting adventure for young John in Totternhoe and Dunstable two thousand years ago.

ADVENTURE ON THE KNOLLS:
A Story of Iron Age Britain: Michael Dundrow.
Excitement on Totternhoe Knolls as ten-year-old John finds himself back in those dangerous times, confronting Julius Caesar and his army.

THE RAVENS:
One Boy Against the Might of Rome: James Dyer.
On the Barton Hills and in the south-east of England as the men of the great fort of Ravensburgh (near Hexton) confront the invaders.

Further titles are in preparation.
All the above are available via any bookshop, or from the publisher and bookseller

THE BOOK CASTLE
12 Church Street, Dunstable Bedfordshire, LU5 4RU
Tel: (01582) 605670